THE FINAL SHOT

A Team's Destiny

Authors

David J. Yarbrough
Dan Garth Haskell

Order this book online at www.trafford.com
or email orders@trafford.com

Most Trafford titles are also available at major online book retailers.

Printed in the United States of America.

ISBN: 978-1-4269-5029-2 (sc)
ISBN: 978-1-4269-5030-8 (e)

Trafford rev. 12/27/2010

 www.trafford.com

North America & international
toll-free: 1 888 232 4444 (USA & Canada)
phone: 250 383 6864 ♦ fax: 812 355 4082

Dedication

I dedicate this book to all the cancer victims and survivors, also to their families and loved ones that have been affected by this ugly and terrible disease. We need to lean on our family, friends and our faith during these troubling times. It is my hope and prayer that a cure will be found and that we will no longer have to suffer from this disease they call "Cancer." Dan Garth Haskell

I dedicate this book to all survivors, and to my son, Kristoffer. Like the stories in this book, sometimes I can feel him guiding some of my shots.   David J. Yarbrough

May we all learn from the lessons taught to us by the 2005 Tooele Basketball Team and their coaches. David and Dan.

Contents

Acknowledgements and Credits

This book is filled with stories and statements that were discussed with the authors by many coaches, athletes, parents, sportswriters, and our many friends. We especially want to acknowledge their contributions to this work and thank them for searching through memories, scrapbooks, and sports memorabilia to share their experiences with us and the reader.

We especially want to thank Karrie Palmer for keeping a fantastic scrapbook. Dennis Workman for his clear memory, Mike Holt, Taylor Palmer, Colton Hogan, Coach Charlie Mohler, Coach Dan Medina, Coach James Brown from Snow Canyon, Coach Lonnie Magnusson from Wasatch, Sportswriter Nick Drake, well known author Gerald N. Lund, and Jordan Biorge for the book cover design.

Introduction

Although the setting of this story is Tooele, Utah and more specifically in the midst of purple and white colors at Tooele High School, it doesn't matter where you attended school. It doesn't matter what the names of the characters in the story are or if your mascot was a white buffalo. You can just as easily be a mustang, a stallion, a cowboy, a wildcat, or any other mascot. This story is about life, compassion, and athletic achievement. This is a true sports story.

The goal of this story is intended to be of a personal nature that will inspire each one of us to become a better person. The message is delivered to us by an underdog comprised of fifteen boys, five assistant coaches, and their head coach. They started out as individuals then worked to become a team who loved and respected each other. The team was plagued with setbacks and surrounded by an unending array of naysayers and skeptics. The players and assistant coaches were embarking on a journey to learn the essential character traits that give life eternal significance. For their head coach it would become love for his players, his family, and a battle for life itself.

Tooele (pronounced tuː'ila) is a city in Tooele County, an estimated 32000 residents live in the Tooele City area.

The unusual name for the town is thought by some to have evolved from an old Ute Indian word for tumbleweed. This is only one of many explanations that cannot be verified because the name was used before the introduction of the tumbleweed (Russian thistle) to the United States. Other explanations claim that the town was named in honor of a Native American chief, but controversy exists about whether such a chief ever lived. Others hypothesize that the name comes from "tu-wanda", the Goshute word for "bear", or from "tule", a Spanish word of Aztec origin that means bulrush. It is doubtful any of these ancient possibilities that predate the settling of the old west is the true origin of the name "Tooele."

For centuries, Tooele Valley has been the indisputable home of the buffalo and the mightiest beast of them all is the white buffalo. Therefore, it is fitting that the White Buffalo was chosen to be the mascot and symbol of Tooele High School.

Tooele County begins on the south end of the Great Salt Lake and reaches from the ridgeline of the Oquirrh Mountains on the east to the Nevada border on the west. The cross country freeway known as Interstate 80 travels 120 miles through this part of the county. This drive rewards the traveler with a wonderful view of the lake and the historic Bonneville Salt Flats.

Tooele is a name that isn't seen or heard too often in the United States - not to mention the world - but in Utah it is quite recognizable. Most of the association throughout the United States is with several complexes: the premier racing facility known as the Larry H. Miller Sports Park; the Tooele Army Depot where a large area is devoted to storing military ammunition; the Tooele Chemical Disposal Facility which is part of the world's largest storage and incineration site of deadly chemical weapons; Dugway Proving Ground where an even larger area in Tooele County is designated for testing dangerous biological and chemical weapons, and for several incinerators and permanent storage pits which handle toxic waste that has been dumped in Tooele County from all over the world. Good and bad can be said about the way these vast areas of land are used.

Little good can be said about one very noticeable atrocity, the continuous scars of ugly gravel pits that mar the entire base of the Oquirrh Mountains. As soon as drivers exit either Interstate 80 or Interstate 15, on the east side to enter Tooele County the ugly pits dominate the view.

The winters are cold and the summers are hot. In either case, to see the real beauty of the county it is necessary to go inside the canyons or out into the extensive high deserts. Tooele County is very large and the residents have found many opportunities for recreation. Bird refuges, historic sites, horseback riding, cycling, hiking, fishing, hunting, skiing, rock hounding, picnicking, camping, racing, land speed trials, off road vehicles, and rodeos are enjoyed. Regardless of the give and takes, the local residents love the good and adapt to coexist with the bad.

The residents of Tooele have success and aspirations like everyone else. Unlikely success comes to people in all walks of life, not just in sports. No matter what is important in our life there is always the possibility we can triumph over the giants that surround us. After all David did slay Goliath.

More recently, a fun story illustrates how the mighty continue to learn from the weak. The controversial Cassius Clay, who later became known as Muhammad Ali the greatest boxing champion of all time, was once told by a flight attendant to fasten his seatbelt. He quickly replied, "Superman don't need no seatbelt!"

The unimpressed flight attendant was just as quick with her reply, "Superman don't need no airplane either."

Muhammad Ali needed to be told to fasten his seatbelt just once and he never compared himself to Superman again. He wasn't quiet in the future but he moved on, "If you can do it, it ain't braggin'!" He had a lot to say that included another one-liner, "I'm so fast I can turn out the lights and be sound asleep in bed before the room gets dark."

Athletics is fun, serious, and an important part of life throughout the world.

In the history of Tooele, many respectable achievements have come from alumni of Tooele High School. There have been many athletes but there have also been scholars, scientists, musicians, artists, politicians, businesspersons, and much success in all walks of life. This isn't about them or the joys of the county. This is a sports story.

Chapter One
Answer the Call

Know ye not that they which run in a race run all but one receiveth the prize, so run that ye may obtain.
1 Corinthians 9:24

In Utah it is not unusual for all four seasons to be felt in the same day, especially during the month of April. In 2002 this was one of those days. Early one morning a blizzard was howling outside but shortly after lunch the sun was shining brightly. Gary Alverson was relaxing at home sipping a tall glass of ice water with a splash of lemon. He was drifting in and out of daydreams and real sleep in the quietness that surrounded him. At fifty-seven years old he was one of an elite few that could relive championships that spanned five decades in athletic events he had participated in as a player or a coach.

Or, he could reminisce about past and present religious activity with the same interest. Of course, if the truth was really known, he wouldn't be thinking about games that had been played - he would be thinking about future games. In fact, as he dozed, he probably wasn't thinking about sports at all. The most important love in his life was his beautiful wife Lois and his family.

A telephone rang in another room until it was answered by Lois. A few moments later she handed it to him with a cautious look of optimism. "Yes," she said, "Gary is right here." Due to excitement she nearly fumbled the hand-off to her husband.

Gary spoke on the phone for a few moments with a look that changed from hopeful to a countenance that got brighter until he could no longer hide the thrill he was feeling inside. The only words Lois could catch him saying into the receiver were "Thank you, yes I will." Then, "thank you," again. He set the phone down and opened his arms out wide as he turned to look at his wife.

Needing no more encouragement, and understanding everything her husband had to say before he could say anything out loud, she ran into his open arms. They hugged each other tightly and turned around in a circle until Gary was able to speak. "I have the job in Tooele." Then they laughed and hugged each other again, with tears forming in their eyes as they celebrated the joyous news together.

Gary had already enjoyed a successful career teaching and coaching in high schools. Most teachers his age were content to spend retirement checks and have some free time. But his work was not complete because for more than thirty years he had waited for the opportunity he wanted most: he wanted to be the head coach of the Tooele High School (THS) basketball team. He had graduated from THS thirty-eight years before and even taught and did some assistant coaching there immediately after college. When the head coaching position opened he applied for it but he was passed over. Determined to become a head coach, he faced one of the toughest decisions of his life and accepted the job elsewhere. It was heartbreaking to leave his alma mater where he had excelled in sports and served as the student body president but he was determined to return.

During the subsequent thirty years he applied for a head coach position at THS on at least three occasions. His persistence finally paid off; he could return to the school he loved most. He would put every ounce and fiber of energy both mentally and physically into this opportunity as head coach of the boys' basketball team. His priorities were firmly established; family first, religion second, and then the Tooele High School Buffaloes.

Gary couldn't wait to get to the THS basketball court and his new classroom. He knew the school building was brand new but the reality hit him like a rock when he rolled to a stop in the parking lot. The old gymnasium, where Gary had played, had stood next to the old high school building for what seemed like forever but both were gone, replaced by a modern athletic center inside the new Tooele High School. He leaned over the steering wheel to look up and down the new walls that stretched far to the left and even further to the right. The new building was indeed a modern day marvel.

He didn't know what fate awaited him as the new head basketball coach at THS but he expected it to be the greatest experience in his life. As if it was just yesterday, in his mind he could see the exciting games he had been part of in the old gymnasium. The muscles in his knees and arms flexed when he relived jumping to grab a rebound before spinning around to throw a full court pass to a teammate for a fast break layup.

He thought about several games and fun times that occurred in the old high school. There was a lot to remember; one thought led to another and they were all good. He sadly realized there was nothing he could do to add to the history of the old brick buildings that had been torn down or to bring volumes of forgotten memories back for thousands of alumni. That wouldn't feel natural to him anyway. On this day the old school basketball programs became a thing of the past too. After all, he was making the decisions for THS basketball now and he was ready to move forward with his plan and some new goals to achieve. He would bring THS basketball into the twenty-first century to match its state of the art educational facility. He was back at the school he had never forgotten. "I can do it," he said out loud as he locked his car door and picked up his briefcase from the asphalt. Beginning on this day, Gary would be known as Coach Alverson to all Buffaloes or as he would say, "The kids just call me Coach."

Gary, like many alumni, learned from this reminder that times we thought would never end do and eventually the old three story brick building that housed those times would be gone. But we also know some things never change. If you have had the good fortune to be a student, a faculty member, an administrator, an employee, or even a friend or a family member of one of these individuals from Tooele High School your heart is forever and forever in Tooele. You are a true White Buffalo.

> *Victory belongs to the most persevering.*
>
> *Napoleon*

> *The future belongs to those who believe in the beauty of their dreams.*
>
> *Eleanor Roosevelt*

Chapter Two
Glory Days

Our memories of yesterday will last a lifetime... These are the best of times.

The Best of Times--Styx

The THS Buffaloes have won a flurry of state championships in swimming and wrestling, and they have been state champions in soccer, baseball, football, and softball. Some years have been better than others but the boys and girls have always been competitive. Success in boys' basketball brought region championships in 1953, 1970, and 1993 but never a state championship. It has been more common for THS basketball to perform in the middle of the pack.

One of the great football teams from Tooele played in 1962 and our future basketball coach was a player on that team. In a newspaper report about an important game that season a term surfaced that has seldom been used. The term refers to an emotional level when excitement and unity reach a crescendo among all true Buffaloes that is nearly uncontrollable. During this instinctive moment in time a mystery occurs that compels the THS Buffaloes to form "the herd." Then the herd stampedes forward with extreme determination, passion, and teamwork as a united force composed of athletes, faculty, students, and the community to capture an impossible goal. It's a powerful and unforgettable feeling that occurs so rarely most students go through high school without an opportunity to experience it.

A *Deseret News* staff writer, Joe Liddell, recognized the fever in 1962 when he wrote about the herd. This is the report in the style used nearly fifty years ago. If you listen closely while you read the article you can hear the captivating voices of Buff sports announcer William "Bill" Gochis and Joseph "Joe" Leonelli, his assistant, on the old KDYL-AM radio station in Tooele. The name Gary Alverson is also mentioned.

Tooele Tramples Hillcrest Crew for 30-0 Region 4 Title Win

BY JOE LIDDELL

TOOELE- Like a starved thundering Herd, Tooele's stampeding White Buffaloes broke loose in the second half of the tilt on their own gridiron Friday and routed Hillcrest 30-0.

The victory gave "The Herd" the final stamp on the Region 4 championship two full games ahead of their pursuers, Murray, who loses Friday afternoon 14-13 to Jordan. Another one point squeaker in the region saw Cyprus sink Granger 20-19.

The title was the Buff's third since Coach Dean Stringham started with the Tooeleans nine years ago. They play East High's Leopards (who partly filled Tooele's bleachers Friday afternoon scouting the contest) next week in the state tournament semi-finals.

Hillcrest kicked off…Wham! Bill Lamb! He caught the boot on his own 30-yard stripe, got a vital block in front for him by teammate Gary Alverson and seven seconds later was across the losers' goal for a touchdown.

Gale Bailey intercepted a long Hillcrest pass on his 34-yard mark. Four plays later Ken Colledge aerialed from the losers' 44-yard mark to Alverson on the 15 and he ripped five more yards. Colledge kept the ball on the next play and raced untouched around the left end to pay dirt. Eddie Dalton's boot made it 16-0

Jim Leonelli gobbled in a bouncing interception again on a deep Hillcrest pass to Tooele's 30-yard stripe and came back to the 39. The losers shoved the Buffs back twice but Lamb took a pitchout and galloped 40 yards to the Hillcrest 10. Another penalty against the winners and Colledge looped to Alverson in the end zone the first touchdown after the start of the fourth period.

Steve Bunn caught Dalton's 25-yard heave into the end zone later after a 15-yard penalty. Final, 30-0.

Tooele went on to win the state championship that year, which was admirable, but it was for football. Earlier in 1962, basketball had dominated sports with excitement all across the state of Utah and throughout the United States because the number one college player in the country and a two-time All-American was playing at the University of Utah. His name was Billy "the Hill" McGill.

He was from a high school in Los Angeles when he arrived at Utah with a rattletrap knee -- the result of a high school injury -- he was good enough to lead the Utes to the Final Four in 1961. He was also good enough to score sixty points in one game and score in the fifties in three other games. He even scored in the forties in nine more games.

McGill recorded the four highest-scoring games in Ute history and six of the top eight. He also notched the two highest rebounding games (twenty-four and twenty-three) in school history. Every gym, school yard, and driveway basket in Utah was filled with kids who were rebounding, blocking shots, and driving to score while they thought about Billy "the Hill" McGill.

One of the greatest moments in Utah sports occurred on Feb. 24, 1962 in a game with BYU on their own court in Provo, Utah. On that night in Provo, McGill set a Utah record that has never been broken. He scored sixty points in a single game. The game was listened to by hundreds of high school students on transistor radios throughout Utah.

Billy McGill was a great "money player" who led teams to championships with his athletic ability.

Later that same year in 1962, when a great Tooele football season was going into the record books the mood was escalating rapidly in anticipation of another basketball season.

Unfortunately the basketball seasons at THS, in 1962-64, failed to enjoy the success of the football team or to add heat to the basketball fever burning throughout the state. The games were exciting but the problems in Tooele continued beyond the 1964 season. Billy "the Hill" McGill had gone into the pros as the number one draft pick in 1962 but a new sensation named Dick Nemelka, a Utah athlete from West High School in Salt Lake City was tearing up the courts for the BYU Cougars. Basketball was aflame as Utah's number one sport and the high school teams throughout the state were fueling the fire. It was a frustrating year to have a struggling team.

This time a *Deseret News* staff writer named Norm Sheya published a written report about a basketball game which pretty much described another tough season for the Buffaloes. Gary Alverson was mentioned again, but this time there was no mention of "the herd." Alverson was wearing a white jersey with a purple number 55 stitched on it. He scored nineteen points with his teammates Medina scoring sixteen, Poulson fifteen, Lewis eight, Sharman three, and Warner two.

TOOELE TIPS GRANGER, 63-60

BY NORM SHEYA

GRANGER- Granger and Tooele met Tuesday in the Lancer gym to decide who would be the cellar dweller in the Region Two basketball standings.

Tooele won 63-60. Granger is alone at the bottom.
Neither team liked the haunting thought of occupying last place.
The count never had more than a six point spread and the screaming crowd stood for the last two minutes.

Granger fans didn't like what they saw as Tooele's Bob Poulson sank two foul shots with 12 seconds left for the victory.

The first half was a nip and tuck affair. Near the end of the half a blanketing Granger pressure unnerved Tooele's guards; Granger scored three goals for a 36-30 lead at intermission.

Second half was more of the same. Forward Gary Alverson put Tooele ahead with a jump shot at the third quarter's end.

The fourth quarter continued like a Hollywood script, the lead changing with each turnover of the ball.

Tooele's John Medina and Alverson and Granger's Joe Winrow, Jim Paulk and Steve Davis were spectacular in the frantic, closing minutes.

But it was Poulson's poise at the charity stripe that put Granger at the bottom of the cellar.

Be strong in body, clean in mind, lofty in ideals
James Naismith

Chapter Three
My High School

Know this, that every soul is free
To choose his life and what he'll be.
For this eternal purpose is given
That God will force no one to heaven.
Know This, That Every Soul is Free
—Anonymous Hymn

Coach entered the high school a full hour before the buzzer to kick off the new school year in August 2002. This would be the first year in the new building. He was amazed that everything really was new to him. All of the teachers had changed and he recognized very few names from the old Tooele families. None of the students knew him. He felt like he was in a fish bowl when he walked in the hallways, towering head and shoulders above the taller students and in the ozone above the shorter ones. He became accustomed to the stares from students who looked surprised and some who looked afraid but he smiled and nodded at them all. He loved it, he wanted everyone to be happy, and it wouldn't take long to become friends with them. That's just the way he was.

He had organized his classroom with family and athletic photos. The normal flags and customary posters that depict history and government were displayed befitting a history classroom. About twenty-eight students were expected to attend each class period. The first buzzer sounded like an evil reminder as most of the eyes lifted to search the ceiling to discover where it came from. The room became perfectly quiet when the buzzer stopped and Coach stood up behind his desk to tell his name and a little bit about his history.

He instructed the students to take turns standing up, to look at the other students, state their name, and asked them to add anything they wanted. Each student did stand to state their name before sitting back down so fast it was a blur. Then Coach continued to describe the goals of the class and what he expected the students to accomplish in his class. The classroom remained quiet for the entire period. The Tooele students appeared to be absolute angels. When the next buzzer sounded no one looked up, instead the students appeared to be pulled by a powerful magnet straight toward the door into the hallway. This continued through every class on the first day of school.

When the day ended, he had no basketball players to mingle with because most of them were practicing football, so he went straight to the football field. Being careful not to disrupt the practice or distract any of the boys, he casually walked to the bleachers and sat on the third row at the thirty-five yard line. Within a few minutes he could tell the Buffaloes had an excellent football team.

The first game was in two days and he would not miss it. For most of the season he continued to observe the practices from a distance. One boy at a time became associated with him until he learned every boy's name and they knew his. They called him "Coach." He knew football as well as he knew basketball but he never stepped across the line to intervene in any way. He was excited just the same. When he spoke about the potential of the football team he wouldn't hold back. "We can win one!" he would tell them referring to a state championship. That's just the way he was.

On the second day of the history class the buzzer to begin sounded again. This time there were no eyes looking up, few students were sitting at their desks, and the buzzer could barely be heard above the confusion. Coach had been here before too, as the cliché says, "this ain't my first rodeo." He picked up a notebook then started walking down the first aisle. When he approached the first rowdy student he said the student's name then wrote it in his notebook. They stood side by side until the student quietly sat down. He moved to the next rowdy student, then the third and the fourth, doing the same. After four, the majority of the class was seated and attentive so it wasn't much longer until the few remaining felt conspicuously out of place and calmly settled into their desks. Coach was back in control.

The students were very impressed that he had memorized the names of everyone during the short time since the first class. He explained to them the importance of a winning team. A team consisted of every player and every coach. "We are a team," he admonished them. "If we fail to work together no one will achieve all that is possible." He made them laugh and he encouraged them to respect him because he was a gentleman, a competitor, and excited to be their friend. There were moments when the students behaved like teenagers but they liked him so they remembered where they were. For every situation that occurred in the classroom Coach had a response that he had practiced time after time for many years. He was prepared and well organized. Of course, it didn't hurt to have the student's names already listed in his notebook in the order they were seated in his classroom to begin the second day of school.

A professor during Coach's days at Snow College had warned the potential teachers not to be misled by the perfect little angels on the first day of the school year. They were always good on the first day because they were watching the teachers very intently and sizing them up to detect what they could get away with. But the second day would be the worst day of the whole year when the students tested the teacher to see if they had detected the teacher's weaknesses correctly. This proved to be a valuable lesson.

Some additional advice was given to the future teachers by the wise old instructor at Snow College: "A few of the students will say some insensitive remarks that will hurt your feelings very badly. When it happens, remember you are their teacher and there is nothing different you can expect from students who hurt their parent's feelings the same way. All you can do is forgive them, forget about it, and then move on."

Two football players always watched for Coach so they could visit whenever possible in school or at the football field. The boys were gifted athletes in every type of sports much like he had been in high school. They were Kyle Brady and Matt Holt; both were on the THS basketball team that he had basically inherited from the preceding coach. They were in great company when they were together.

The 2002 football season was phenomenal; the Buffs had three rough games then blew everyone away through the rest of the season, through the state tournament, and then beat Wasatch for the state championship. Wasatch was one of the three teams that beat the Buffs early in the year; in a real barnburner; but the Buffs won the game that counted. Coach posted a clipping from the newspaper in his classroom showing Matt Holt leaping to catch a touchdown pass in the championship game.

Kyle Brady had earned honorable mention all-state and all-region as a sophomore; first team all-state and region MVP as a junior and a senior; Utah 3A MVP as a senior, and 2002 Prep Star Western Region first team. When the 2002 season ended the Buffs had won a state championship while Brady had rushed for 1400 yards; caught passes for 700 yards; became the state's career interception record holder with thirty-one, scored twenty-eight touchdowns, and he made fifteen interceptions during his senior year. He was team captain in football and basketball. He lettered in baseball and track and made first-team all-state and all-region in baseball. He was on the honor roll and named Utah's 2002 "Mr. Football."

Tooele was Sports Town, USA to Coach. THS was where he wanted to be: "We can win one!"

In 2002, Tooele had won the State Championship in football but as in the 1960's their basketball team continued to have a tougher time. They ended the season in 2003 with nine wins and twelve losses and the 2004 season finished with an unimpressive record of twelve wins and ten losses. During both years they had improved slightly but a new coach doesn't have his complete stamp on a team until his third and sometimes fourth year.

Right from the start he told his assistants, "We will win a state basketball championship if it takes ten years but we may not have that long. We can win one. I won't retire from this job until we do." They made adjustments and implemented new procedures to use in practice. They searched for new looks in talent, physical conditioning, mental ability, and character traits. During 2002 to 2004 the environment and style that began at the junior high school level was adapted to the philosophy and basketball programs taught by Coach. Every aspect worthy of development was used to guide hundreds of boys forward in life and toward the varsity basketball team.

The new direction was grueling and demanding. Very few boys had the desire, stamina, and determination to endure to the end. It was fun but challenging and it made the players feel good physically and deep inside. The next varsity team would be chosen entirely from the new coach's training program. The players would be the boys he wanted and he wouldn't want to trade any of them for another player. He would be held accountable for its success and accept full responsibility for the team. Coach was anxious to play basketball.

The basketball season for 2004-2005 began with the usual expectations that didn't give the Buffaloes much of a chance to break even with wins and losses. Fortunately, there was some added interest in the Tooele community because Coach was in his third year and had led another Utah high school (Bonneville) to win a pair of State Championships in 1985 and 1987.

There are many roads to a state championship. But the road most travelled is the one when that one in a million player suddenly flares into existence on the basketball court to try out for your team like a Josh Grant, Shawn Bradley, and Kendall Youngblood. All three were Gatorade Utah High School Basketball Player of the Year Award winners. In fact, the new coach knew this road to the state championship well because Kendall Youngblood was his "money player" in both the 1985 and the '87 state championships and they narrowly missed two more championships in1986 and '88. After the long and grueling tryout period, which stretched late into the fall of 2004, hopeful players had endured several cuts to reduce the roster, the final cut was made.

If the 2005 THS team somehow came through with a decent season it would surprise everyone. This would be a long season with a very young team and it was rationalized away quickly by calling it another rebuilding year. It was too early to tell whether it was an alibi or a prediction but it was duly noted by the experts anyway. The naysayers didn't predict or even hope for a Gatorade or any other Player of the Year; they just had three seniors who may not be among the team's starting five. They doubted the team would have a good year and said a lot of luck would be needed just to win enough games to break even.

Coach Alverson announced the names of the players who made it past the final cut to be on the team. The boys may have been young but they had reasonable talent, and probably of more importance their mothers had taught each one of them to be obedient and respectful. They were smart, unselfish, and coachable.

Throughout the history of Buffalo basketball, regardless of the season outcome, being a THS basketball player has been a very high honor for every boy that has ever been on the team. When Coach selected these boys they immediately felt the awe of responsibility that came with the honor. Coach had experienced the same honor at THS and he had lived a life of example to accept the responsibilities that came with it. They were innocent young men and he knew how they felt.

Soon after the selection, Coach met with his new team. He said important things to motivate them and he took some steps to become their friend. He ended his remarks by sounding like every coach in the state who was dangling a state championship in front of his players and assistant coaches as encouragement: "We can win one!" he told them. The future was unclear but the team had been set in stone. It was time to begin the 2004-2005 season and the rosters for the games would include:

Players:

3	Zack Connelly	5'11"	Junior
4	Josh Cedar	5'10"	Junior
5	Nash Lockie	6'3"	Junior
10	Mike Holt	5'11"	Junior
12	Dorian Cochran	5'7"	Sophomore
14	Josh Johnson	5'10"	Sophomore
15	Bryton Lawrence	6'2"	Junior
23	Josh Boucher	5'10"	Senior

24	Tyler Cheatham	6"4"	Junior
33	Cody Castle	6'4"	Senior
34	Colton Hogan	6'5"	Sophomore
40	Alex Despain	6'3"	Senior
44	K. C. Huffman	6'4"	Junior
45	Mike Trussell	6"7"	Junior
50	Taylor Palmer	6"3"	Junior

Coach Dan Medina

Coach Charlie Mohler

Coach Chris Ashby

Coach Phil Merino

Coach Chris Baker

Head Coach Gary Alverson.

I don't have any tricky plays, I'd rather have tricky players.

Abe Lemons

Tooele High School
Varsity Basketball
2004-2005

Row 1
Mike Holt.Zach Connelly.Josh Cedar.Josh Boucher.Nash Lockie.Josh Johnson. T.J. Witkowski.Dorian Cochra

Row 2
Bryton Lawrence.Tyler Cheatham.Taylor Palmer.Cody Castle.Mike Trussell.Colton Hogan.Alex Despain.K.C. Huffma

Coaches
Coach Medina.Coach Mohler.Coach Ashby.Coach Alverson

Chapter Four
Practice

*It makes me be a little wiser and it makes me work a little bit
harder so thanks for making me a fighter!*
Fighter—Christina Aguilera

The Tooele coaches loved practices. Day after grueling day the players
practiced offensive and defensive plays, again and again. It didn't seem
that there was much focus on basketball fundamentals but there was
certainly a high priority placed on learning and executing the offensive
plays that eventually would be called during the right situation in a real
game.

Defense soon became even more significant. During games defense
was meant to be the focus of every player from the tip off until the final
buzzer, regardless of the score. Coach convinced them that the better
they played defense the more successful they would be on offense. He
also taught that defense dictated the tempo of the game. This team would
practice defense so much that it became their dream at night.

The fundamentals of dribbling, passing, running, and shooting had
come naturally to the coach when he was a youngster. Maybe he believed
these fundamentals and some of the other instincts of the game were
basics the players should possess naturally or at least develop on their
own. Whatever Coach was thinking didn't alter the fact that his team

would have a procedure or a play for every situation that arose during a game. "Run the play, one more time," he would shout at least a dozen times before the end of practice. Then, as usual, he would find numerous opportunities to issue his reminders: "keep your head in the game;" and "be a leader; don't follow. I don't want followers; be a leader!"

Coach understood that this team did not have a "money player" to provide the coattails for team members to ride on. He needed every player to stretch his abilities, to understand the technicalities of the game, and to be able to accomplish his assignments when he was on the court. He needed every player to be a leader on his team; a team of players with traits that would make any one of them the leader on any other team. This team would face disaster if the players watched and followed whoever they considered to be the best player. If he could inspire his players to grasp this concept then he could make up some of the ground that was lost on fundamentals that required years to develop in addition to a lack of experience and a full schedule of games filled with very stiff competition.

At the end of each practice the players were sore and tired but they encouraged each other. They loved it. They became friends and buddies on and off the court. Although they wanted to win, they weren't concerned whether the future blessed them with a win or a loss, great statistics, or an award.

The night of the first game finally arrived on Wednesday November 24, 2004. Tooele traveled to Price, Utah to meet Carbon in a non-region matchup. The Buffs appeared more pumped up than nervous and jumped to a six-point lead at the end of the first quarter then a thirty to sixteen lead at the half. In the second half Coach cleared his bench to make it possible for eight players to score. It was an important opportunity to give his players some game experience and a chance to calm some of the pre-season jitters. The team exhibited good teamwork with a stand out game by Josh Boucher who scored seventeen points which included fifteen points coming from five three-pointers. The game ended 63 for Tooele against 50 for Carbon.

Carbon High School is a smaller school in a lower region classification but they were known for hard work and being a persistent team. It was a good test for Tooele and they began their season with an important win. They felt a little less pressure after getting into the win column without any losses. Even though it was very late, the van ride home was filled with happy and smiling faces of young men who had too much energy to sleep.

Winning the first game was important but Coach wanted the team to improve defensively. He felt that fifty points were too many to allow the Carbon school to score so the upcoming practices consisted of a few offensive plays, shooting, learning a matchup zone defense, and a lot of defense.

One week later Tooele played at home against a bigger school than Carbon. The Kearns Cougars were also one win with no losses. Coach quickly implemented a matchup zone defense that bewildered and frustrated the fast Kearns team. The Buff's defense limited them to eighteen points in the first half while Tooele poured in thirty-four. In the second half Coach cleared his bench again which made it possible for nine Buffaloes to score. This time it was Mike Holt, a junior, with eighteen points including four three-pointers, who led in scoring.

Defense was the name of the game however, allowing Kearns to score just thirty-four points during the entire game. Unable to penetrate the Buffaloes relentless and perfectly executed zone defense the Cougars were forced to bomb away over the top from beyond the three-point line. The bombs turned out to be duds, scoring just one three-pointer per quarter totaling just four three-pointers in the entire game.

The frustrations of the Cougars were compounded by a barrage of points scored by the Buffaloes at the other end of the court with well executed moves straight from the coach's playbook. Tooele won with the score, Tooele 59 against Kearns 34. The Tooele High School Buffaloes moved to 2 wins and 0 losses.

Basketball is a game that is often compared to life. Some good things happen but often there are bad things that happen too. The qualities and character that make a good basketball player are also the attributes required for a happy and successful future. A player can develop many great characteristics to become an excellent performer on the court but he will never reach the highest pinnacle of success until he is willing to accept the gifts the game of basketball offers to him. In the end, thousands of hours and untold resources are lost unless the individual accepts the same traits, as gifts, back from the game to exhibit in his or her personal life that they have put into the game. Great coaches and true champions at all levels of competition understand this principle and maintain a healthy perspective about the game and the importance of life.

Just two days after the Kearns game, Union High School came to town to test the Buffaloes on their home court. Both teams had just one day of rest and one very limited practice. Union struggled throughout the game without ever enjoying the lead. Their facial expressions gave the impression they didn't want to be on the court. They even appeared to feel miserable when they had the ball on offense. They scored just fifteen points in the first half. Tooele won the game as a testament to good defense, especially by Cody Castle. The team improved their record by winning their first three games. The final score was Tooele 57 against Union 43. Tooele had eight scorers in the game and for the third time in three games there was a new leading scorer as Cody Castle cashed in for thirteen points.

Four days later on Tuesday, the team played their third game in seven days. Tooele traveled to Woods Cross to meet some resistance that the team had not yet seen. On December 7, 1941, Japan carried out a sneak attack on Pearl Harbor that brought the United States into World War II. On December 7, 2004 a brutal series of bombs hit the Buffaloes. Many of the bombs were included in the scoring of Bryson Riddle, a "money player." To add to the shell shock, Woods Cross unleashed an intense defense to match Tooele's, which appeared to weaken and slack off a bit.

At the end of the first quarter, Woods Cross had held the Buffaloes to just six points after averaging sixteen points per first quarter in the first three games. In reality, the Buffs didn't slack off as much as it appeared by the final score. Instead, it was the eight three-pointers that rained on them above their zone defense against just three three-pointers by the Buffaloes. Tooele fell behind five points in the first quarter but the Buffaloes fell just two more points through the second, third, and fourth quarters combined. Bryson Riddle was the first "money player" Tooele had encountered this year. Riddle scored twenty points.

Tooele and Woods Cross both left the court with 3 wins and 1 loss as Woods Cross had won a battle against a team of Buffaloes that played tough right down to the final buzzer. The final score was Woods Cross 50 and Tooele 43. The high scorer for Tooele was Mike Holt with fifteen points. An important story for the Buffaloes was that Nash

Locke, another junior, had his fourth consecutive offensive performance in double digits by scoring eleven points in this game and eleven, ten, and eleven in the first three games.

After starting the season with three wins in a row the loss showed the Buffs the staggering reality that basketball is indeed a game of wins and losses.

A review of the schedule for Tooele warned the coaches that as the season progressed the competition would get stronger. There was no time to delay so Coach Alverson took advantage of the two days available for serious practicing, Wednesday and Thursday. A day of travel to Castledale on Friday for an evening game against Snow Canyon High School in the Coal Country Classic would be another physically demanding day for his team. The coach knew that after their first loss to Woods Cross, the two full practices, and then the long ride to Castledale his team would face a very tough task of matching up against the tall, talented, and very experienced Snow Canyon team.

The three hour trip in the team van to Castledale was comfortable and uneventful until the quietness was interrupted by the coughing of Coach Alverson. He had been coughing occasionally since the school year started but on this afternoon the coughing spells were frequent. The assistants made some comments to Coach that they were concerned about the viciousness of the attacks. Coach shrugged off the comments but he couldn't hide the coughing. Some of the spells were so difficult for him that when they finally ended he was seen gasping and holding his chest to catch his breath. Then he would groan quietly to himself as if the coughing had been very painful. It was obvious to the assistant coaches and the players that he needed to see a doctor.

The Snow Canyon Warriors were well rested with a "money player" of their own, 6' 10" Coby Leavitt, and they were a powerful team that ranked number three in the state. Tooele started strong by staying with the Warriors through the first quarter with twelve points apiece. By halftime the Buffaloes fell six points behind at 24 to 18. By the end of the third quarter the Buffaloes lost more momentum and fell behind 39 to 28 which would be too much to deliver in the fourth quarter. Coby Leavitt put the final nail in the Buffs' coffin during the fourth quarter by pouring in ten of his seventeen points in the game.

Surprisingly, the attention grabber for the two game event of the evening was Mike Holt who thrilled the crowd by scoring the game high for all four teams with twenty points. This was also the third time in five games that Holt was the high scorer for the Buffaloes. The game ended 57-45 in favor of Snow Canyon.

The next night, December 11, twelve players scored for Tooele to win the consolation bracket at the Coal Country Classic. The scoring included eleven three-pointers in a rout that doubled the scoring of the Park City Miners, 76 to 38. Tooele had four wins and two losses.

Snow Canyon beat Emery in the tournament championship game to advance their record to 5-0.

Tooele always has had some very dedicated and enthusiastic fans who are true purple-and-white dyed-in-the-wool of Buffalo basketball junkies. Many times the magnitude of their interest in the high school basketball program has gone unnoticed by the school administrators but when the team came home from beating Park City, a rumbling began to stir in the community which strongly supported an action by the administration that they did not anticipate. The administration was surprised when approval of the new coach became so evident. Somehow they were caught believing it was going to be another season filled with the usual THS basketball. The new coach and his team were up to something that was ramping up interest but the administrators could not agree on how, when, or what it was. Meanwhile, this year's young team was looking respectable and next year was looking promising. Maybe the day would come when the rest of Region 11 would take the THS Buffaloes a little more seriously.

Alverson had been the Buff's coach for two full seasons. They were the typical so-so seasons at THS with the usual mediocre win-loss records. As expected there had been some thrilling wins and some embarrassing losses but all of these games were with a team of players that Coach Alverson had inherited from the last coach. With that in mind, the fans in the community were among the first to recognize Coach had put some of his touch on the team to show some obvious improvements during both the first and second year.

This year the team that had already won four times in just six games was totally his team. He made the final decision to pick them and it was his responsibility to develop them. It was a team known to be young with the majority of the team returning as seniors, next year would be when THS should become a powerful force. Although it was impossible this year, a small stir of anticipation was brewing that next year Coach Alverson and his team might win the fourth Region Championship in its ninety-two year history and they would even have a fair chance to look tough in the 3A State Championship Tournament.

Many of the fans remembered Coach because of his athletic abilities in basketball, football, baseball, several track and field events, and when he was Student Body President of Tooele High School. Several records he set have not been broken. The surrounding area was filled with residents who not only remembered Gary Alverson - they loved him. People who weren't in the Tooele area back in the early sixties had listened for two years to stories about his athletic performances, as well as the examples of integrity the coach had displayed as a teenager, so they were beginning to warm up too.

A long list of outstanding male and female athletes can be compiled from many different sports at THS. Even basketball has had so many fantastic players it is futile to attempt to name them all. Drew Hansen played at the University of Utah and went to the NCAA Championship game. Doug Tate played at Westminister and Brett Applegate played at Brigham Young University, both were powerful athletes with great careers. But the legacy left by Gary Alverson was jumping out of the historical archives to be reintroduced to the present generation of sports fans. THS had waited for a superior team since basketball began in 1913 until 1953, then until 1970, then 1993, and now another twelve years for a basketball team to have an outstanding season. If it ever was going to happen again, the time couldn't be better. Coach had come home.

On December 15, THS went to West Valley City to play Hunter High School. They fell behind six points at halftime. Swanigan a "money player" from Hunter was on fire scoring twenty-one points but the Buffaloes played with another team effort to come from behind to win 64 to 57. This time it was Taylor Palmer who was team high scorer with sixteen points and the fourth, different, team scoring leader in seven games.

December was barely half over and the region games had not yet begun but there was a wide range of confusion about where the present young team at THS, with five wins and two losses, fit into the schematics of state, region, and even THS basketball. The optimistic believed they would outperform their expectations to make it to the tournament but they would not go all the way to win the state championship. A few more believed they would perform well within Region 11 but it would be difficult to do much more. However, most fans and experts believed the team would win four or five of the ten games during region play.

The Buffs had one day to prepare before travelling to another away game against the Logan Grizzlies. Coach Alverson did his best to prepare the team with a long and very intense practice but with limited time most of the burden would be left for his team. He hoped his team would recognize and adapt appropriately to the Grizzlies game plan without forcing him to use timeouts that might be needed later in the game.

During the shortest days of winter practice began in the afternoon after school ended and continued until well after dark. The players came to school in the dark and went home in the dark. In the freezing parking lot after a long practice one of the players appeared to be exhausted and happy the session was over. An alert assistant coach who observed the player couldn't resist the opportunity to yell above a few cars, "Hey, what do you think about basketball now?"

The surprised boy didn't want to respond with a comment that admitted he was tired so he wisely looked at the sky before yelling back, "Basketball is great, coach, but I was wondering why every time we practice, it gets dark!"

The next game with the Logan Grizzlies began and immediately after the tip off the Buffaloes demonstrated patience by playing a ball controlled offense and scored often. On the other end of the court a tenacious zone defense provided them with a 37 to 25 lead at the end of the third quarter. During the fourth quarter, Riley Nelson, the "money player," for the Grizzlies ripped the nets to score most of his twenty-one points but the Buffs held onto the lead to win a squeaker on the road, 47 to 43. Coach was very pleased with the equal distribution of points scored by his team with Nash Locke scoring the game high with fourteen.

They say that nobody is perfect. Then they tell you practice makes perfect. I wish they'd make up their mind.
Wilt Chamberlain

Chapter Five
Running Wild and Free

I was eight years old and running with a dime in my hand into the cafe to pick up a paper for my old man. I'd sit on his lap in that big old Buick and steer as we drove through our town. He'd tousle my hair and say, "Son take a good look around, this is your hometown."
My Hometown—Bruce Springsteen

With one game to play before Christmas the main topic of conversation throughout the valley continued to be the new and very improved basketball team at THS who had a respectable record of six wins and two losses. The conversations were supportive but filled with apprehension about how the new coach would continue the surprises. The intense competition in the upcoming region games would surely increase the pressure on his young players as the season progressed.

One of the biggest basketball fans and a close friend of the new coach was the wrestling coach at THS named Dennis Workman. He had known Gary Alverson when they went to elementary school in Stockton, a small town south of Tooele. Dennis was excited to discuss his friend and share his obvious respect for Coach.

With a big smile and a laugh Dennis took a deep breath as he gathered his thoughts then he began to share his memories, "Gary graduated from THS in 1964. When he was born his family lived in Stockton. It was my hometown too, and we loved it. I was actually a few years younger than Gary but we attended the elementary school in Stockton together back when there were less than sixty students in the first through the sixth grade. Everyone in the small school knew each other very well especially the boys who were always in a group playing athletic games together. Most of the time the games were baseball, basketball, dodge ball, or a soccer game that we modified to play on the elementary school yard using baseball rules.

"As a kid in elementary school Gary was already taller than everyone else, at least a full head taller. He was faster, a better player at everything, the most fun to be around, and a friend to everyone. He was also the best organizer so we depended on him to organize everything. He would get all of us together to play whatever sport was in season. When it was baseball season he rounded up every boy in Stockton to hike west of town then cross the railroad tracks to play baseball on a flat piece of property that was owned by a man in town named George Bryan. Mr. Bryan also owned the town's only operating gas station on Main Street.

"Outside of being flat about the only things that resembled a baseball park were a few weathered boards that had some rusty chicken wire nailed to them to create a small backstop. During these summer games there was no shade and we were nearly a quarter of a mile from the nearest water but we spent hundreds of hours there and we had fun. During those years we had several excellent baseball players and we won several minor league baseball championships in the county. Our team was named Odd Fellows which was a well known fraternity back then. Today, the Elks, Eagles, and Moose are similar organizations. Undoubtedly, Gary was the best player.

"Gary organized the dodge ball games, the modified soccer games, and basketball games, that we played on the school yard. Actually the place on the school yard where we played was a large cemented area that was intended to be a tennis court but none of us could ever remember tennis being played there or ever seeing a net. Like I said, I was a few years younger than Gary but I was naturally bigger than the other boys my age and I was pretty strong too so I was always invited to play in the games that Gary organized. It made me feel very happy to be considered a player good enough to play with Gary and the older boys.

"Most of the time we played basketball for several hours after it was dark and until it was late at night because the tennis court had lights. Many of the nights were in the winter with the snow trampled down on the cement in a larger and larger area as we got closer to the baskets. Sometimes we wore so much clothing to stay warm that it was difficult to pass or shoot the basketball very far, but we had fun.

"Several years later, probably after I became an adult, it finally dawned on me that Gary was a very smart organizer who knew my father was the Town Marshall. He knew if he invited me to play basketball with him and the older boys that I would bring the electrical fuses that the Town Marshall controlled at his home to operate the lights on the tennis court!

"I remember when, four older boys from Grantsville, probably already out of high school, came to Stockton to chase some of the Stockton girls. As far as I know they only came to our town once. Gary lived across the road from the tennis court when a few of us elementary school boys spotted them and realized what they were up to. The older boys had parked their car across the street from Gary's house just outside the tall woven wire fence next to the tennis court. It was during a hot summer so the boys were stretched out inside the car listening to their radio with their car windows down.

"I don't want to tattle on anyone or mention any names but a good organizer came up with a plan to fill water balloons with water then charge the car with as many water balloons as we could carry. According to the plan we would throw all of the balloons through the open windows to soak the boys inside the car. The next part of the plan was to use the element of surprise in our favor so we could turn and run to safety. The plan was so well organized that it worked perfectly for most of us. When the wet Grantsville boys jumped out of the car they quickly noticed that Gary was the fastest runner so three of them went after him in hopes of surrounding him so they could pin him down. That left one of the older boys to chase after the rest of us in a different direction.

"It wasn't long until he caught me which left no one to chase the rest of the Stockton boys so they all ran to safety. As I suspected, none of the three older boys would be fast enough to catch Gary so I was the only boy in our group of five or six to get caught. The Grantsville boys asked me to tell them my name which I did. When they heard my name one of them asked if Paul and Billy Workman were my older brothers. They apparently knew them from playing against them in high school football. They were both big and both of them were very strong. When I replied that I was Paul and Billy's little brother they turned me loose. Not even one us was hurt for soaking those older Grantsville boys inside their car so I have always believed that the organizer truly did develop an excellent attack plan that kept the rest of us from getting hurt, even if we did get caught.

"During the last week of elementary school the boys participated in a pentathlon that consisted of a fifty yard dash, throwing a shot put, high jumping, broad jumping, and shooting a basketball. Everyone's performance was evaluated using a sophisticated coefficient like a handicap to put every boy on equal footing. The coefficient worked against Gary because he was taller, a sixth grader, and he had an excellent height versus weight ratio on the charts. It didn't matter, Gary still performed so much better in every category that he scored well above everyone in our elementary school, all of the junior high schools in the county, all of the rest of the elementary schools in the county, and all the rest of the state. He just kept on winning. After the coefficient took a whack out of his score, he was still in first place in all of those faraway places!

"Neither Gary nor any of the rest of us had any idea that the pentathlon would be important so far away from our sixty student elementary school. We just wanted to beat each other and Gary did his best by giving it everything he had to beat the rest of us. Soon after that some important person took him all the way to Colorado to compete in the Pentathlon there. Gary did his best by giving it all he had again. He won the region. All of us were between eight and twelve years old so we didn't know what the Colorado Region was. We just knew it at least meant most of the United States or maybe the world. This was the beginning of Gary's achievements in sports. His talents kept improving, expanding, and surpassing others even until now.

"Several dozen of us were seriously heartbroken when his family moved away from Stockton to Henderson, Nevada down by Las Vegas. It was like moving to another planet back then. Gary was twelve years old. We missed him, I know I missed him a lot and I thought about him often. Luckily our silent prayers were answered, I guess, because one year later the Alverson family moved back to Tooele. This was good since all of us, who were old enough, rode a school bus to the same junior high and the same high school where Gary was anyway.

"In high school Gary was on the football team that won the state championship, he was also on the baseball and track teams that took second place in the whole state. He set records on the track and field team in several events and some of them are still THS records today. Amid all of this effort and all of the time involved in sports he was also successful as the student body president. He was friendly, fair, and concerned about every student whether it was sports or another worthy aspect of life. The student body loved him.

"I was a freshman when Gary was a senior and the student body president but we had been very good friends for many years. He was a very good friend of everyone. One day, I remember waiting to get on the school bus to go home after school. Another boy who was a senior purposely knocked a towel out of my hands when he walked by me which caused my wet towel to unroll and spill my swimsuit onto the ground. Being big for my age and stronger than most high school boys I pushed the senior. Even though I was just a freshman we were pretty equal in size.

"I knew the boy too, so after we countered each other back and forth a few times with just pushing and shoving it appeared to me that the altercation wasn't going anywhere. Like a fool, I stopped pushing then walked a few steps before bending over to pick up my towel and swimsuit. As I looked up, bam, the senior popped me on the jaw and knocked me completely out. When I came back into existence a few moments later all I could see was my school bus preparing to pull away from the curb. The senior who hit me and his buddies were long gone.

"No matter how much I hurt there was nothing I hated worse than missing my bus ride home because in those days missing the school bus meant you had to walk seven miles to get home. As I attempted to coordinate my efforts I remember Gary and another student hurrying to help me upright myself. They did not see the altercation but they recognized I needed help. Gary quickly brushed the grass and dirt off my clothes then he pointed me toward the school bus. I felt his hand on my back as he gave me a gentle shove toward the bus. I continued to run toward the bus while he was jumping up and down, waving his hands wildly above his head, and yelling at the bus driver to wait for me. That is the way Gary was then, feeling good about himself and wanting everyone else to feel good too. That is just the way Gary is now."

Dennis continued, "In the late sixties most of the boys who were older than eighteen would "rustle" to earn money at the International Smelter that was located on the side of the mountain on the east side of town. The smelter has been torn down for quite a few years now. Back then a roster or roll call of employees in many of the different departments inside the smelter was used to determine the number of positions that were not manned for the shift. That number was reported to the "rustling room" where the unemployed males over 18 were gathered in hopes of being selected to work that day.

"When a full time vacancy occurred the replacement would be chosen based upon his performance when he had been a successful rustler and the number of shifts he had been successful rustling. The smelter paid a very good wage that was as competitive as or better than any place in the surrounding area. The wage was much higher than the minimum wage jobs that were filled by most of the high school and college students.

"I didn't like to work at the smelter because it was a very dusty, a harsh, and a dangerous environment. And they didn't care too much about safety other than providing a hard hat and steel toed shoes. The smelter became the main source of income for Gary who needed to earn money in less time than required by a minimum wage job. His schedule was already so full it was not possible for him to accept a full time job that would interfere with his school work and athletics. Rustling at the smelter when he could fit it in provided a good option for him. He could earn a good wage. He could rustle for a job on a shift or day anytime he was available or he could be scheduled to work full time when he didn't attend college during the summer. Gary worked at the smelter a lot."

Dennis could have continued complimenting his lifelong friend, Gary had hundreds of friends anxious to do the same, but Dennis decided to direct the conversation to more recent events. "I could not have been happier when I learned that Gary had been selected to become the new head basketball coach. In the early 1970s, Gary was elated to come to THS right out of college as an assistant coach but the school district administrators failed to keep him by not giving him a chance when the coaching job was opened, so he eventually had to go someplace else in order to use his skills and knowledge in a job he always wanted.

"As head coach, Gary won the championship in state high school basketball twice at Bonneville High School which is something the THS basketball program has not done once in more than ninety years. He attempted to come home to coach just a few years ago but the school district administrators denied him again.

"Gary is still an organizer. In his private thoughts, I believe he has planned his life with goals and priorities that he wants to accomplish. He will do all that he can possibly do to accomplish those goals and one of the goals he must have made nearly forty years ago was to cast his talents and example on the THS basketball team to make them great. I may not even know how many times the doors were shut on him during the thirty-five years prior to becoming the head coach of the THS basketball team. But I do know that he didn't give up. He has come home now and he will do his best by giving it all he has." Then Dennis wrapped it up, "That is just the way Gary is."

You see things; and you say "Why?" But I dream things that never were; and I say, "Why not?"

George Bernard Shaw

Never look down on anybody unless you're helping him up.

Jesse Jackson

Coach: Bill Diehl

Back row left to right; Mike Webster, Dennis Workman,
George Anderson, Darrell Smith, Unknown, Gary Alverson.

Front Row left to right; Danny Edwards, Delayne Jacobs,
Ron Edwards, Lynn Allie, John Diehl, Glen Roach, Kent Baker.

Chapter Six
Distraction

One by one, little problems build up and stand in our way.
Right Now—Van Halen

Juan Diego High School was a Class 2A school but they had an excellent basketball team with a very impressive record against the bigger Class 3A Schools. It was unknown at the time but the Eagles would move on to win the State 2A Championship. They had high hopes of catching the Buffs napping instead of taking them as seriously as they should. The game was played in Tooele but there was no evidence that a home court advantage was helping the Buffs in any way.

The Buffaloes didn't resemble the organized and patient team that had been impressive throughout the preseason games. This deviation from their game plan proved to be frustrating and chaotic for them. The Soaring Eagles caught the Buffs napping alright by staying close in the first quarter. They hit the Buffs hard during the rest of the game to win with a final score of 48-42.

After the loss Coach admitted his team didn't execute or play well as a team. "We didn't play very good, especially offensively," the coach noted. "They didn't score that much on us. We just played really poor and not very good basketball. This was the worst game we have played all year and at home. We were not happy with it, nor were the kids.

There was the distraction of the holidays and a lot of other things too. This was the last day we could do anything and now we go to play a game without any practice.

"I think they've had time to think about their performance," the coach added. "Sometimes we don't execute well because our timing is off and our timing is off right now. Those are types of things that can be remedied with practice. But that is the frustration about the holidays when you're not allowed to practice during the moratorium. At least everyone else has to do it too. It will be interesting to see if the team responds. We go to the E Center to play Taylorsville, a big 5A school who has had some big wins so it will be a real challenge for us."

After the game his comments that "the holidays can be distracting to a basketball team" didn't have much importance. But it was the rest of the comment, "there were a lot of other things too," that would soon prove to be a colossal announcement. A simple phrase that slipped by everyone without any meaning. A phrase that was destined to seriously impact the lives of everyone that would witness his team in the future, especially his kids.

Unknown to everyone but a very few, Gary had received the results from some x-rays and medical testing that discovered a rare form of cancer in one of his lungs. His doctor called it mesothelioma. He had never burdened any of his teams by discussing personal problems and he didn't intend to burden this team with the discovery of cancer either. He had been diagnosed in November and had been contemplating how and when to tell them. He told the team just before the game with Juan Diego. Even though one of his biggest concerns was that he did not want the news to be a distraction to the team, he felt that this was a big part of the "there were a lot of other things," comment he had made to the reporter after losing to Juan Diego.

After he underwent his first chemotherapy treatment and realized how sick and exhausted it made him, he knew he had to talk to his team. In an interview conducted a few weeks later he spoke about this dilemma to a local newspaper reporter. "In the event that I was unable to show up for a practice or game, I wanted my team to know why I wasn't there," explained Coach Alverson. He was very concerned about the effect it would have on the team that he proudly referred to as "my kids."

Prior to the Christmas break, the violent coughing spells were often observed by the other coaches, students, faculty, and the team. He knew the treatment sessions were long as well as physically demanding so he may be late or possibly absent from a practice or ballgame. This was a big distraction that he wanted to avoid but he couldn't postpone the inevitable any longer. Eventually, he decided to tell his assistant coaches. The surprising announcement had a crushing effect on them and they instantly recognized the critical reality that Coach and his family must face. It was a sadness they would never forget but they remained composed and offered some words of encouragement to their best friend. Then they discussed how and when to tell the players.

In his usual humble and positive manner he made the decision to let the team know he had a problem with cancer prior to the Juan Diego game and before the Christmas break. This would allow time for the players to be alone, to cushion the impact, while there was a holiday moratorium imposed on practices and before the schedule of region games started.

The boy's varsity basketball team alternated days with the girl's varsity team between the large and small gyms for practicing. The biggest difference between the two locations was the seating capacity. When the boys were assembling in the small gym the assistant coaches gathered them into a small group. Coach took over for a very brief meeting by telling them he had been diagnosed with cancer that may affect his attendance due to the required therapy sessions. He was calm, to the point, confidant, and appeared to be as healthy as ever.

The boys were attentive and appeared to understand but the significance didn't seem to be threatening or worrisome. Especially after the coach motioned them onto the court while he said a phrase they would often hear, "I can beat this."

On December 28, Tooele met the Taylorsville Warriors at the E Center in West Valley City. The Buffs, who had looked so bad the week before when they played Juan Diego, a Class 2A team, appeared to have gotten past the distraction caused by Coach's announcement to make a 180 degree turn. They were playing strong against a Class 5A team and leading the Warriors by nine points at the end of the third quarter. The Buffs had played their ball control offense and tenacious defense brilliantly.

Nearing the end of regulation play the Buffs lost focus, possibly due to distractions, and made a couple of costly miscues that included three missed foul shots that were the front end of one and one situations. The Warriors had stayed within striking distance to take advantage of these opportunities and they overtook the Buffs in the final moments to win the game, 44-42. The Buffs lost a close game but to play in the E-Center was a valuable experience they would never forget.

In every high school gym throughout the state the walls behind the baskets were fifteen feet away at the most. No bleachers were needed behind the baskets for a high school game in the E-Center so it was strange for the players to see emptiness at the ends of the court where they usually saw walls. This caused them to miss some free throws and even shoot some air balls when they normally would have done better but it was a learning experience they would build on.

Colton Hogan broke into the ranks as the high scorer for the game by scoring eleven points; along with Taylor Palmer a junior who had eleven points. Hogan was the fifth player on the team to be the high scorer in a game for the Buffs who had played nine games. Their record was now six wins and three losses.

Coach was very proud of his team and it was obviously a very close friendship with the team when he shared their disappointment in losing. "We played well until the end of the game," he said. "They were able to steal the ball and score in transition. We led nearly the entire game until the end. It was a disappointing way to lose a game. We had a shot to tie the game at the end but we missed. We also missed some key free throws that could have tied the game as well. It was a game that we let get away from us."

After the games had started in December, the practices had been less frequent but more intense when they were dispersed among the nine games they had already played. Basketball life was very demanding. Several games required traveling long distances to places in Southern Utah and then Northern Utah to Logan High School. It was about as far north as they could go in the THS basketball van.

During the holidays, the basketball team had finally earned some quiet time to be alone. They could think about their recent games, the fast moving practice sessions that actually had begun during the previous summer, and they could think about other things too. They had basically lived on the court for months with the same players they had played basketball with for many years. While other boys their age were out looking for a wink from a young girl's eye they had been in the gym listening to the swishing sound of a net.

A short vacation from school and basketball during the Christmas break was a refreshing opportunity to reevaluate their thoughts and drift back into the world of the living. Surprisingly, girls were not the main thing capturing their attention. Each player had a different subject stored in a cavern in his mind that needed some attention now that he had some time alone to sort it out. What is cancer? What is it like to have cancer? Do people recover from cancer? What is it like for the family members of someone with cancer? The meaning of the questions was undoubtedly important to many people and staggering to think about in addition to opening the door for more questions. It was a time for serious reflection. These were somber moments for the players and the questions were powerful. The answers had to be found, not only by the players, but eventually by many History students in Coach's history classes and the rest of the high school students too. All of them were Gary's kids.

As anticipated, 2005 began right on time to end the holidays. To the dismay of a few students the school buzzers were also, right on time. But most of the students were happy to be back in school with their friends, especially Coach who could not have kept himself away any longer. He was ready for practice, there was work to do, and there was a game coming up soon. He wanted to get going.

The news about Coach Alverson had an immense impact on the teachers too so they studied to learn about mesothelioma. The math classes, PE classes, music classes, language classes, science classes, and every other class taught at the high school had solemn-almost secretive discussions about cancer. Within a few days each one of the players and enough students in the high school had learned about the disease to give the appearance that Tooele High School was the foremost authority of all high schools concerning a rare form of cancer called Mesothelioma.

Then the next phenomenon begun when the students learned about his history and the high character that Coach always had. As they learned about him they witnessed a courageous example that deservingly continued to grow into the future. Every honorable accolade that can be used to describe a friend was justifiably attributed to Coach Alverson. That was just the way he was.

Many residents in the community joined the students to become fluent in the language of mesothelioma. At any time, in any location you could hear it being spoken: "The main cause is the inhalation of asbestos fibers. These fibers enter our body when we breathe. The fibers travel to the lining of the lung and cause scarring of the lungs which eventually become either cancer or asbestosis. That isn't cancerous, but it is bad and may turn into cancer."

Tooele County had become the largest classroom in the school district and mesothelioma had become the most unpopular subject.

Coach was sure that his exposure occurred from breathing asbestos when he worked at the International Smelter in the late 1960s and the early 1970s. The smelter was located about four miles from the high school. According to the medical evidence concerning mesothelioma, "The tumor growth in cases of people inhaling these asbestos fibers does not show symptoms until about thirty years after the exposure to asbestos. The longer or more intense the exposure of the asbestos is felt on a person, the greater are the chances of him suffering from mesothelioma. Even people who have worked in asbestos factories for just a few months have been affected by mesothelioma many years later."

Coach was diagnosed in 2004, which is slightly more than thirty years after his exposure to asbestos at the smelter. It may be that his clean lifestyle and good physical shape delayed the mesothelioma. He was always healthy, strong, and active then suddenly without any warning, and just as loud as a gunshot to start the 440 yard race, he had cancer.

The most troubling words from mesothelioma was yet to come, "Mesothelioma takes most of its toll on the human body before the symptoms occur. The average survival period of the people diagnosed to suffer from malignant mesothelioma is usually about one year. The symptoms of mesothelioma are similar to other common diseases like fever, nausea, sudden weight loss, chest pain, and breathlessness. These symptoms are common for so many illnesses that it is difficult to diagnose mesothelioma at an early date.

Mesothelioma causes the protective lining, or mesothelium that covers all the major body organs, to function abnormally and invades the main body organs like the heart, lungs or abdomen and damages them. There are mainly three types of mesothelioma — pleural mesothelioma is the name of the type that affects Coach Alverson. Of the three types, pleural mesothelioma is the most common type and it affects the lining of the lungs. The other two types of mesothelioma cancers affect the lining around the heart and the lining of the abdominal cavity."

The Center for Disease Control (CDC) counted 18000 deaths in the US over the seven-year period from 1999 to 2005, with 2704 deaths in 2005. The disease is rare but the number of malignant mesothelioma fatalities is rising year to year in rough proportion to the population: the annual death rate has been steady at about one death per fourteen per million people in the United States.

The knowledge spread throughout the state like wildfire. It was not comforting but Coach Alverson certainly was not giving up. He had told the players that he had talked to several others who had beat the same cancer and he knew he could beat it too. "I can beat this," he said as an echoing reminder.

During this 2005 basketball season, BYU hired a new coach named Dave Rose. Coach Rose was well known as a player, coach, and an expert on the many facets of basketball and the attributes of life. Those who know him say he has a special way to communicate with his players. He is a great motivator and instills confidence that enables individuals and his teams to play at the highest level of the game.

In June 2009, a fight against cancer became life threatening for Coach Rose and his family. A battle became a personal necessity. After surgery he was diagnosed with pancreatic neuro-endocrine tumor cancer. As he became more involved with his treatments the cancer was reevaluated to be serious but more manageable and slower growing than they originally believed but these were frightening discoveries for his family, the many lives he influenced, and the myriad of people who adored him. The BYU basketball team was very concerned and wanted desperately to help their coach but they didn't know what to do so they dedicated themselves to playing better. As a result the team ended the season with the best record in the long history of the school.

As soon as possible, emergency surgery was performed to remove the tumor and no other cancer has been found since then. All periodic scans since the surgery by doctors at the Huntsman Cancer Institute in Salt

Lake City have come back clear. The United States Basketball Writers Association recognized Rose for his valiant efforts by presenting him the Most Courageous Award. Coach Rose is one of the determined survivors that inspire other victims of cancer, "We all know someone who has or has had cancer and hope they will be the one to beat it."

I would rather have a mind opened by wonder than one closed by belief.

Gerry Spence

Obstacles are those frightful things you see when you take your eyes off the goal.

Henry Ford

Here is a test to find whether your mission on earth is finished: If you're alive it isn't.

Richard Bach

Chapter Seven
Dang the Luck

You can spend your whole life buildin' something from nothing.
One storm can come and blow it all away. Build it anyway
Do it Anyway—Martina McBride

Like friends and family of cancer victims everywhere, the students at Tooele High School felt helpless too. How could so many kids feel such a strong relationship with someone and then be unable to help. There must be a way to help Coach beat the most cruel and unfair adversary in his life! They must be able to do something. They searched frantically in optimistic desperation to find a solution that must be out there, somewhere.

After school resumed there were a couple of days before the next ballgame which would be the final preseason game. Coach conducted practice on each of those days. At the beginning of the first practice after announcing he had cancer, silent anticipation filled the gymnasium as if a completely new routine was about to begin. The team stood motionless like they didn't know what to do but the coach looked energized. He looked healthy. He looked happy and he was anxious to start another one of his vigorous practice sessions. He was just like he always was. A different change was occurring they could not see. Although it was unknown to the team, the time had come for them to learn the fundamentals of life from their best friend. They were about to embark on an unforgettable journey through the glory days of their basketball career with Coach Alverson. Several minutes went by that seemed like an eternity and then suddenly, he said just what they expected him to say, "You bet we have work to do, so I am here to practice. I am not going to sit down and die! I can beat this! Now let's get busy; someone throw me a basketball. This season is not over. We can win one!" They watched him for several moments before they realized there was nothing that had changed in the practice routine. That is just the way he was.

Tuesday afternoon, January 4, the THS basketball team climbed into the van for the fifty-five mile trip to play the highly touted and the very talented Lehi High School Pioneers. The game was a scoring brawl with the lead changing back and forth throughout the game. Lehi led by three points after the first quarter and by two points at half time. Tooele led by four points after the third quarter and by two points with twenty seconds remaining before the final buzzer. But the Lehi Pioneers quickly hit a layup to tie the game. They finished the game with three free throws in the last nine seconds to secure a come from behind win against the Buffaloes. The final score was Lehi 54 and Tooele 51.

A "money player" from Lehi named Ben Walker scored twenty-six points for the Pioneers. The Buffaloes finished the game with balanced scoring from the team that included Holt with fourteen points, Lockie with fourteen points, and Boucher with eleven points.

For two consecutive games the Buffs had lost the lead in the final minutes to lose . When Coach Alverson was interviewed after the game, it was déjà vu all over again and sounded like a repeat description of the game a week before. Coach said his team played exceptionally well but they just can't seem to finish off our games with victories down the stretch.

"Our kids played hard and we led throughout most of the second half," Coach stated. "We missed some key free throws and turned the ball over several times to allow them to get back in the game. We played well against a good team that is expected to win their region and we played on their home court. That is encouraging, but the way we are finishing the games is not encouraging, it is a concern."

Soon after the loss, THS Principle Mike Westover met with Coach. He had fought through some wicked chemotherapy treatments that had left him very fatigued to the point that it was difficult to move. The treatment portion itself lasted six hours but so far he hadn't missed a single opportunity to be with his team. After a brief discussion that included the game, Principal Westover encouraged the coach, "Keep your head and chin up."

Coach didn't exhibit discouragement; instead his response was just as encouraging to the principal. "Just wait and see," Coach replied with a nod and a positive smile.

The third loss in a row brought the Buffs to six wins and five losses to end the preseason games. This loss also opened the cage door for the naysayers in the world of high school sports in Utah. Although it was long before the last game, alibis were surfacing to rationalize another ho-hum season. The six wins and five losses even let the wind out of the sails for many die-hard Buff fans who began to moan; the team was young, the team had distractions, and the important Region 11 games that were scheduled to begin would surely create a darker picture for this year's basketball team.

THS basketball was back to the same-old, same-old again; encouraging moments, exciting games, some frustrating losses, and a mediocre six and five record. The season was at the halfway point and halfway to matching the same unimpressive record as last year with 12 wins and 10 losses but even that didn't appear to be possible.

The last nine games had been an emotional rollercoaster ride. The games had come at them in rapid succession. They won some; they lost some, and just as fast as they moved from hot to cold so did many of the fans. This ride didn't even take into consideration the other distractions that had become so important. When the team won a game they enjoyed the thrill of success together and when they lost they learned more respect for each other.

Practice session in the THS gymnasium was a place of refuge away from the storms that were brewing on the outside. The atmosphere was calm and positive. The peacefulness was a welcome retreat from distractions that accompanied a six and five record. Coach was in his usual form talking about the upcoming region game against the Ogden Tigers on the Buffs home court and coaching toward his goal that was still unclouded. He was still going to win a state championship. The team heard him say, "We can win one!"

So many coaches intend to take the high road only to succumb to the heat of battle. In game after game the pressure finally causes coach after coach to utter words or exhibit an action that cause the game and life to lose the proper perspective. After losing three games in a row many of them go ballistic, especially if one loss was to a 2A school on his home court and the next two losses were when his team blew the lead in the final seconds after leading most of the game.

Coach was not like that. He never said anything bad about anybody or about any member on his team. He never said anything bad about other things either, not even cancer, except that he was going to beat it. He appeared to erase bad games from his memory as soon as they ended so he could move forward from 0 - 0 to get a perfect record by winning the next game. The past was over; what became important was today and the future. When his team was experiencing rough times he was the utmost gentleman who treated his team with respect, as though it was an honor for him to have each one of them for a friend. A poem in a picture frame contains the same words that the players and assistant coaches were witnessing in real life with their head coach. The author is anonymous or at least not identified;

Dear Lord, guide me as
I try to coach this team;
to build each player's character
and boost their self-esteem.
May I keep an even temper
and remember it's just a game.
Let me not have favorite players,
but treat them all the same.
Grant me patience with them
as I praise them or correct,
remembering that I must work
to earn each one's respect.
Lord, whether we may win or lose
may all who are watching see
the kind of coach at every game
that you would have me be.
Amen

Hundreds of boys had grown up during the previous sixteen or seventeen years who played basketball for thousands of hours in hopes of being on the THS basketball team. One by one a boy dropped out of the basketball programs until the final cut on the roster to end tryouts was almost unnecessary. The players who remained continued to impress Coach that they didn't dwell on the past, statistics, or any type of recognition. His team loved to play, they did what he asked them to do, they listened to him, and he knew they would not give up. The deep respect he had for his players and assistant coaches was not measured by wins and losses.

In his mind, he believed this team could be molded into one of the best defensive teams in the state and he instilled the same thought in the minds of his players and assistants. He knew that with perseverance, the Buffs could become one of the best overall teams in Utah's 3A Classification. He also understood that the team was not there yet, but there was still time. .

Fault finding is like window washing. All the dirt seems to be on the other side.

Author Unknown

If you give into your emotions after one loss, you're liable to have three or four in a row.

Chris Evert

A tough day at the office is even tougher when your office contains spectator seating.

Nik Posa

Chapter Eight
A Secret Meeting

We won't be sad, we'll be glad for all the life we've had and we'll remember when.

Remember When—Alan Jackson

Soon after the team returned to school from the holiday vacation, an overwhelming feeling had overtaken each player that was kept hidden inside. The feeling grew until it reached a point they were displaying clues that became recognizable to each other. They had lost three straight games since Coach had told them about his cancer.

Upon investigation, they learned that each one of them was experiencing a feeling of weakness that they couldn't describe. It was like they were being directed to do something. The bottom line was they needed to discuss it together as a team privately to work it out, without the coaches. So they arranged to have a secret team meeting.

The atmosphere in the meeting was very humble and so reserved that the locker room seemed almost like a spiritual sanctuary. It didn't show, but deep inside the boys were disappointed about losing the last three games because they felt as if they had let their coach down. It wasn't the losses that concerned them; instead there was a voice deep inside, more important than basketball, whose whispering was becoming forceful.

As the meeting progressed, every team member commented that something must be done to help Coach; he had become the most important person in their life. As individuals they felt helpless but maybe as a team they could do something to help him. Within minutes they agreed there was nothing they could do about his cancer. Then just as quickly they agreed that their Coach would do better against cancer if they could steer his interest toward something else that would keep him mentally and physically strong.

As young men who knew their best friend very well it was obvious that each one of them must change his attitude and step up. They must win the State 3A Championship as a team. In addition they must develop and exhibit the same character traits exhibited by their coach in order to accomplish that goal. During the short meeting, each player dedicated himself to accept the call to step up in character and pledged to win the state championship for Coach. It would be a mission of destiny and they would be a "Team of Destiny."

There was not even a needle in a haystack, let alone one that could be found, that would give them a chance in a million to succeed in their quest.

At the beginning of the next game with the Ogden Tigers, it was apparent that three losses in a row had a chilling effect on the expectations and enthusiasm of the fans, but the team wasn't concerned about past performances. No one but the team knew about their secret meeting or the mission compelling them to move forward. To the observers, it appeared that motivation and encouragement was coming from the coaches or their parents to fuel the boys for the game. Many experts were skeptical but no one could predict how the Buffs would perform against a savvy team with a nearly identical record.

None of the Buffaloes showed any sign of intimidation or worry of any kind when they charged onto the court for warm-ups, but they did not exhibit any cockiness or arrogance either. They were embarking on a trail that had never seen this herd from Tooele High School.

Starting with the tip-off the Buffs poured it on the Tigers all night long. They used a hurry-up offense to push the ball into fast breaks down the sidelines when the opportunity was there. If a fast break was not possible they immediately switched to a patient ball control offense with set plays. They displayed a high pressure zone defense, and excellent foul shooting throughout the game. The Tigers were held to 44 points while the Buffs scored 53. Mike Holt scored eighteen and kept the Tigers at bay in the fourth quarter by hitting eight out of nine foul shots.

The performance was pleasing to Coach. He summarized the game by saying, "That is a pretty good team we beat. They are very athletic and they will win some games in our league. It was a huge win. It's always important to get that first win in a league game. We showed some consistency and I really liked our defense. I thought our inside players really played well. Taylor Palmer played a good game. Cody Castle and Bryton Lawrence came off the bench and played well. It was good. We had a lot of people involved in the victory. We improved from the game before. We showed patience and protected the ball and hit our free throws."

Tooele began Region 11 competition with one win and zero losses. In the mind of the coach and his players they had made it half way through the season with a perfect record.

Like every morning for two years, Coach Alverson walked through the front doors of THS then slowly down the hallway as he gave hellos to the students and his fellow faculty members. He made his way down the hall and up the stairs to his classroom. Inside, his students could see photos, plaques, and several relics from his great career attached to the walls and on the shelves. As usual he sat down behind his desk with his head just below a black and white photo of him playing basketball during his college days. He had played on the Brigham Young University freshman team in Provo, Utah and on the Snow College team in Ephraim, Utah. Surrounding that photo were pictures of other teams he had coached and some family photos.

Throughout the day he taught his history classes and walked the halls giving a wave and a friendly eye to those he passed. He was popular with the faculty and students. They enjoyed being near him as much as he enjoyed being close to them.

The students in his history classes were never neglected. Coach obviously enjoyed teaching the subject and the students had as much fun with the lessons as they had with him. One of the classroom activities that they enjoyed was comparing the year he graduated from high school, 1964, with the current year, 2005. On one occasion they were comparing the value of money. He would name an item and its price then the students would answer by giving the current price. Then they would alternate back and forth. He said, "Dow-Jones Industrial Average, 891."

The class responded, "12880."
"Cost of a new home, $20,500."
"$160,000."
"Cost of a new car, $3500."
"$23,000."
"A postage stamp was 5 cents."
"Today they are 39 cents."
"A gallon of gas was 25 cents."
"Today a gallon is $2.35."
"A quart of oil was 32 cents."
"Today a quart is two bucks."
"A dozen eggs was 54 cents."
"Today they cost 99 cents."
"A gallon of milk cost 95 cents."
"Today a gallon is $2.00."
"The average income was $6000."
"Today it is $22000."
"A loaf of bread was 21 cents."
"Today a loaf is $2.00."
"Monthly rent was $115.00 per month for three bedrooms."
"Today rent would be $950.00 per month."
"A movie ticket was $1.25."
"Today a movie costs $6.50."
"A cheeseburger, a shake, and French fries were 75 cents."
"Wow, today they would cost more than five bucks."
"Minimum wage was $1.10 per hour."
"Today it is $6.50."
"Pay for an eight hour shift at the International Smelter was $18.81."
"Today it would probably be more than $20.00 per hour for at least $160.00 per eight hour shift."

This was a fun activity that could be done by comparing many categories in 1964 with 2005. Sometimes the subject might be politics, music, clothing styles, or other news of the day.

There was one seventeen-year-old boy named Darren, who sparked the interest of the class because he claimed that he had never made a basket or hit a baseball anytime during his life. This was unbelievable to Coach and left him absolutely flabbergasted. He just could not believe a healthy and strong boy who had spent his entire life in Tooele had never made a basket and never hit a baseball. Coach had done both several hundred times during recesses in elementary school.

Darren and the coach referred to the claim many times during the first semester. The second semester was beginning with the coach as bewildered as ever. To him, Darren had accomplished an impossible feat so he made a well thought-out comment to him, attempting to entice the boy to answer in a way that indicated he at least played the games. Darren was either honest or very intelligent or possibly both because he never wavered from supporting his claim. "I played marbles during recess in elementary school. By the end of every school year I owned three thousand marbles and a hundred boys in the school owned zero. Then I switched to electronic games," he would say.

Conversations in class with Darren always made the coach smile and shake his head from side to side. Meanwhile, the students were attentive and interested in the humorous banter between the two. One day Coach was relating a story about opening a package from his mother in 1966, when he was in North Carolina. He hurried to prepare a handwritten letter to thank her. When he was proofreading it he noticed there was a line he didn't like but he left it in the letter anyway. Sure enough, his mother misinterpreted the same line when she read it. It hurt her feelings and it made him feel sad for a long time. He learned to be sensitive and careful about what he said and wrote after that.

When he finished the story, Darren raised his hand and Coach motioned for him to respond. Darren simply asked, "Why didn't you just push edit or delete before you pushed send?"

When music was the topic of discussion Coach named a few songs that he thought were popular in 1964 such as, "I Get Around" by the Beach Boys; "I Want to Hold Your Hand" and "She loves You" by the Beetles; "Where Did Our Love Go" by the Supremes, and "Oh Pretty Woman," by Roy Orbison. The class instantly turned to hear what clever comments Darren would have to say. He surprised them by saying, "Hey, that's cool; at least you had excellent music to listen to."

Coach was surprised when he named the popular movies in 1964: Mary Poppins, *Goldfinger, A Shot in the Dark,* and *From Russia With Love.* There was not one student in the class who was familiar with any of these movies and Darren had just one simple question, "Did they have sound and color?"

Often, Darren would be texting on his cell phone before and immediately after the buzzer to begin and end class. The texting led the coach and Darren into a discussion concerning the differences between attending high school in 1964 and attending high school in 2005. Coach voluntarily pointed out, "When I was in high school we didn't have Nintendo, cell phones, computers, iPods, or even digital cameras."

When Darren heard this he went into the same bewildered and flabbergasted act of disbelief that the coach had been using on him. With his eyes open wide, Darren leaned back with both arms draped over the back of his chair. Then he slid down into a slouched position. In dead seriousness he looked up at the coach and replied, "Wow, hadn't anything been invented to do with your fingers back then."

This was one of the heartiest laughs the history class had during the year and the teacher loved to laugh with them.

Basketball gained importance when the coaches and the team mingled with the faculty and the students. They were surprisingly upbeat about the future. These enthusiastic vibes were transmitted throughout the high school then the students spread the excitement out into the community. Pretty soon it was well known that the THS Buffaloes did not have any doors closed on them yet. In fact; the past was old news, what counted were the games in region play, and in region the Buffs were tied for first place with a perfect winning record.

The daily practices continued to focus on plays, shooting, defense, and scrimmaging to incorporate playing time with what the team had learned. The coaches were constantly adding the science of basketball to improve the mental aspects of the game. "The game is not just run and gun and guard somebody," they would shout across the court.

Every situation had a set procedure to react with which required practice. Steals, blocking out, and rebounding were an important part of defense but the coaches began to emphasize, "Touch the ball, get a finger on those shots, get a finger on those passes, and touch the ball when they dribble. Just touch the ball."

On the night of January 12, 2005, people lined up outside the brand new THS Gymnasium from the ticket window around the corner of the building then down the entire length of the parking lot. Many of them were forced to park in the adjacent THS Auditorium parking area and some parked as far away as the junior high school.

Many fans didn't make it into the building. The bleachers, the aisles, and hallways lined with windows above the hardwood court were packed shoulder to shoulder for a game between the two largest schools in the county. The number of Grantsville Cowboy fans who were out in full support for their team as well as the numerous Tooele fans made it evident that previous win-loss records for the season had been thrown out the window. Neither team sported an impressive record but the intensity for this cross county rivalry was as great a competitive event as you could ever imagine.

The game lived up to the hype. In a hard fought game the Buffs used a strong start and clutch free throw shooting against their opponent who came from seven miles to the west. An important lesson was taught to the Buffs by the Cowboys: never give up. This attitude brought the Cowboys back from a 31-14 deficit that the Buffs enjoyed as late as the halfway point of the third quarter. During the previous eight minutes the Buffs had pounded the Cowboys twenty-one to four. The Buffs also put on a classic defensive show that limited the Cowboys to just two three-point baskets at the end of the first quarter. The Cowboys were limited to six points again during the second quarter then scored just one more basket nearing the midpoint of the third quarter but Tooele's big lead was about to be tested.

A burst of scoring from a determined group of Cowboys led by Derek Erickson and Marcus Hamatake brought them back from no-man's land to make it a tight game, cutting down the Buffs' lead 43-40 with 1:45 to play. Grantsville had a chance to take the lead but misfired on two possessions. The Cowboys were on a ride to pull off a great comeback but the clock became their worst enemy by forcing them to foul. Cody Castle hit six out of six free throws during the final thirty-four seconds of the game to settle the score with the Cowboys at 49-40.

Holt had sixteen points and Boucher had eleven to combine for twenty-seven points for the Buffaloes. Erickson had sixteen points and Hamatake had thirteen to combine for twenty-nine points for the Cowboys in a thriller that would keep the rivalry alive.

Coach was both relieved and ecstatic after winning the game, "We played good defense in the first half that made it tough for them to score. We did a pretty good job adapting defensively on them. Holt had a series of five baskets before the half ended which was big. I took Cody off the bench and his free throw shooting down the wire gave us a boost. Our big players complimented one another really well. I like the way our big guys unselfishly play smart, because if they don't have a shot, they kick it back out and we run the offense again.

"Josh gave us a big boost offensively early and got us off to a good start," the coach added. "It was a duplicate from other games, but we've learned from these other games. We've worked very hard at finishing games and keeping our poise and executing. It was a big win for us. We haven't done a lot yet because you have to hold serve on your own court and get a couple of wins on the road to be successful in region."

Tooele's coaches were loaded with compliments for their team. The last five games had demonstrated a serious principle that you never give up. None of the five previous opponents had given up. One game was lost on the Buff's court to a 2A team. The Buffs had big leads in the next four games: they lost two games and had to hold on to narrow leads in the other two games in the closing minutes. Tonight the team grasped the concept before it was too late. The lessons from the past had been discussed and it was time to move forward. The season was just beyond the halfway point and in his mind, Coach Alverson was pleased to preserve a perfect record with two wins and zero losses.

> *One man can be a crucial ingredient on a team, but one man cannot make a team.*
>
> *Kareem Abdul Jabbar*

Chapter Nine
Never Give Up, You Can Do It Too

Better stand tall when they're calling you out: don't bend, don't break, baby, don't back down. It's now or never.

It's My Life--Bon Jovi

A basic component of not giving up is to not lighten up. The boys were succeeding in building a lead during the game, but just when it became apparent they were doing well, they would sub-conscientiously lighten up. The opposing teams were taking advantage of this opportunity to get back into the game. This is a very difficult moment to identify for players and coaches. A coach wonders, do I substitute or should I build an even greater lead. This is a decision the coaches are paid to make. For players the answer is simple, never give up. Give all you have every minute you are in the game. Teams come back from a fifteen or twenty point deficit much more frequently than a twenty point lead is increased to a forty point lead.

A BYU football team beat University of Texas at El Paso, 85 to 7. Jim McMahon was the quarterback for the BYU Cougars. After the game he admitted that time ran out before his team could score more touchdowns and that the BYU defense could have been a little better. McMahon never gave up when he was on the field. Later that year (1980) at the Holiday Bowl in San Diego, it was his team that was losing to Southern Methodist University (SMU) 45 to 25, with just four minutes left in the game. McMahon could have lightened up, accepted defeat, and headed for the National Football League (NFL) but he didn't give up. His teammates caught on fire due to his attitude and fought hard to beat the clock and the seemingly impossible deficit. The Cougars miraculously clawed back to within six points on the final play. They had the ball. McMahon took the snap then threw a Hail Mary pass as far as he could possibly heave the football to a surrounded Clay Brown in the end zone to tie the game. Kurt Gunther kicked the extra point with no time on the clock for the BYU win, 46-45. To this day, it is remembered as "The Miracle Bowl." When you are in the game do your very best, win or lose. Never give up.

Danny Ainge made unforgettable plays as a youngster and throughout his career as a professional player. He was known for playing on winning teams. He had a reputation as a tough and talented competitor who never gave up. His hard play and determined attitude started building in high school when he led his basketball team to back-to-back Oregon state championships and continued to the end of his last NBA game. Naturally, opposing teams found it difficult to play against the only high school athlete ever to be named a first-team All-American in football, baseball, and basketball. The difficulty spread to opponents in the Western Athletic Conference arenas as Ainge became BYU's all-time scoring leader—in the era before three-point lines—all while playing pro baseball for the Toronto Blue Jays.

Word of Ainge's athleticism spread coast-to-coast his senior year at BYU (1981) as he single handedly staged a comeback against a tough Notre Dame team, led by another All-American by the name of Kelly Tripucka. During the thrilling NCAA Tournament game, the lead had changed hands several times. Tripucka made a long bomb to put BYU behind by one point with only 7 seconds left. The Notre Dame fans were jubilant that he had made the last shot of the game. The ball was inbounded to Ainge. He dribbled the full length of the court, somehow slipping past four defenders, and then rolled a beautiful lay in off his finger tips, just out of reach of the fifth player who was Notre Dame's tallest man. All five defenders had taken a whack at stopping Ainge but he scored the winning basket with a play that is still making the highlight reel in NCAA tournaments. At the end of his college career, in 1981, Ainge received the John R. Wooden Award, given to the top college basketball player in the country. Whether he was in a winning or a losing game, his attitude was the same: never give up.

During a practice, Coach had a feeling one of his players was having a personal problem that was unrelated to basketball. The boy's father had died from a heart attack a few years earlier while he was exercising on a tread mill. His mother had remarried a very decent, hard working, and caring man but the boy still felt the loss. Occasionally he had worries and troublesome thoughts that he kept to himself. Even though the boy was well mannered and liked a lot by everyone, he often appeared to drift through the days with no thought about the future. He had great respect for Coach and secretly adopted him as his dad.

Coach arranged a private opportunity to meet with the boy when they could be alone in the gym. "Colton," he smiled as he motioned for the sophomore to come to him. "You have the best no-look pass I have ever seen. Left-handed makes it even more effective!" The young center beamed in delight at the compliment. "But," Coach continued, "I believe you have something besides basketball to talk about." A few moments elapsed to allow him time to arrange his thoughts then he entrusted the problem to his coach. They talked and evaluated the problem for a few minutes until the boy felt better. At the end of a successful and encouraging discussion he put his hand on the boys back while he gently pushed the player to get him running toward the court. Then he yelled some more advice, "Do what I tell you in basketball. If you are moving forward and things don't go right, go left!"

The team continued to practice to develop skill and coordination. They listened to the coaches to develop the mental ability to identify different situations that would arise in upcoming games. Recognition, anticipation, adapting, and reacting were essential mental skills that became tools to be used during the scrimmaging portion of the practice session in preparation for the games. The team was getting stronger on the court but destiny demanded they incorporate virtuous qualities of character into their life off the court as well. Every practice ended on an encouraging note such as, "Think about where you go and always remember who you are." Coach understood the dangers on and off the court. He wanted them to be safe by avoiding potential traps wherever they were.

Students in his history class and the high school were learning some important principles also. "Never give up" meant school, occupation, physical, and religious endeavors. How can lightening up in a homework assignment be a benefit? How can doing just enough work to get by be beneficial for future promotions? Does using illegal drugs and alcohol promote strength and health? Or, I don't do the things that are going on there so does hanging out where bad things are happening mean lightening up on the goal to never give up religious values? Coach's example provided clear answers to everyone. "Always do your very best, make the best use of your time, do not lighten up in pursuing your goals, and never give up!"

> *When I was young, I never wanted to leave the court until I got things exactly correct, my dream was to become a pro.*
>
> *Larry Bird.*

> *Don't let what you cannot do interfere with what you can do.*
>
> *John Wooden*

> *Success is the ability to go from failure to failure without losing your enthusiasm.*
>
> *Sir Winston Churchill*

Chapter Ten
Agony of Defeat

Why don't you hit me with your best shot? C'mon, hit me with your best shot! Fire away!
Hit Me with Your Best Shot—Pat Benatar

The game against Grantsville on Wednesday night had been a drain physically and emotionally. The practice on Thursday didn't slacken off either. Friday, the Buffs were scheduled to travel to Morgan High School. Nothing seemed to get easier for the Buffaloes. Tooele may be thinking they had a perfect 2-0 record but the Trojans from Morgan had a perfect 16-0 record for the whole season.

Morgan routed the Buffs from the beginning to the end in what few spectators even called a ballgame. The Buffs appeared to wander through the game to the beat of five different drummers whether they were on offense or defense. The game seemed to be a lot longer, especially for the Buffaloes, but the Morgan Trojans played just four quarters. As the game progressed the Trojans did not lighten up; they lead Tooele by fifteen points after the first quarter; by thirty-two after the second quarter, by forty after the third quarter, and by a whopping forty-three points at the final buzzer. Tooele made just six baskets in the first three quarters. The final score was Morgan 80 and Tooele 37.

The loss was a devastating embarrassment for the Buffs. After the game, very little was said by anyone from Tooele. A student mentioned overhearing a Morgan fan say they wanted to win by fifty. Maybe the Buffaloes were lucky the clock had been on their side to stop the bleeding. At this time, the Buffs would be happy to win a game anywhere in the state at any level of high school. But the rest of their games were in the region full of teams credited with being the toughest in 3A State basketball.

At practice the following Monday, the discussion was limited to the positive aspects of the game with Morgan. This didn't take much time and was completed quickly before the coaches attempted to move forward. The players continued to struggle with the agony of being beaten so badly. In dismay, a starting guard slipped a profane word that was heard by the coaches. Immediately everyone turned in one synchronized motion to see the reaction from Coach, then they froze.

The gym was so quiet you could hear a pin drop. The facial expressions on fifteen boys and even the five assistant coaches looked like deer in the headlights when a Peterbilt semi-truck loaded with logs was zeroing in on them.

The head coach remained calm with a very slight change of expression on his face, but it was enough to burn iron. They all realized using bad language on his court was serious enough to be corrected. "Let me tell you something," Coach began. "Difficulties in life are intended to make us better, not bitter." Then he very calmly asked, "Do you know any place where saying that word is acceptable?"

The player who uttered the word already felt bad enough but he timidly replied, "No coach, I don't, and I am sorry."

"I will forget you said it," the coach responded to the young man. Then he offered his team some advice, "If you are ever in a place where that kind of talk is acceptable; get out of there as fast as you can!"

Each player recognized Coach meant what he said because he cared about them as a person and he would never lighten up his own ideals to accept profanity under any situation. If it was said in a movie, he would stop watching it. If it was written in a book, he would stop reading it. If it was sung in a song, he would stop listening to it. In a simple but forceful way, he had stood up for what he believed before giving them some good advice about where they should be at all times.

As the practices continued on Tuesday, the emotional hurt from the Morgan game became a nagging feeling that stayed with them. In the game they learned a valuable lesson that the coaches had been attempting to teach them for several weeks. If they had a lead in a future game they would not lighten up. They would play their best to the end, regardless of the score, as if destiny demanded it, and leave the rest up to the coaches. With a league record of two wins and one loss a chance to be in the final tournament was still possible but the future had been seriously darkened by forty-three points. Morgan had hit the Buffs hard and they hit them some more with one shot after another.

The next day was Wednesday, another travel day to a game with the Ben Lomond High School Scots in Ogden, Utah. Both teams were 2-1 in league action but the Scots sported a brilliant 11-3 overall record against an 8-6 record for the Buffaloes.

The Scots took over right where Morgan stopped in last week's bloodbath, scoring thirteen points in the first quarter. Sadly, the Buffs also took over right where they left off against Morgan scoring just four points. At the end of the first quarter in the previous week, Morgan led 20-5. At the end of the first quarter against the Scots the Buffs trailed by nine points at 13-4.

The Scots didn't let up; at the end of the second quarter they increased the lead by another seven points, at the end of the third quarter they increased the lead by another nine. The score to begin the fourth quarter was a whopping fifty-one for the Scots against an embarrassing twenty-six for the Buffaloes. During the fourth quarter the Buffs were able to prove they didn't give up. They outscored the Scots significantly 24-15 but they were far too short. The final score was 66-50. In a pivotal game, the record in league play for Ben Lomond advanced to 3-1 and the Buffaloes dropped to 2-2.

For the second time in five days the Buffaloes had taken the best shots their opponents had to offer and were walking out of a gymnasium filled with exuberant fans into the freezing night air for a long and quiet ride home.

The Buffs were disappointed they let coach down again with another very poor performance. A season record at 8-7 and a league record at 2-2 put them in the same history book Tooele had been in for eighty-nine out of ninety-two years. At practice the next day, Thursday, the effect of two losses on the road of destiny became complicated to them and doubt was tempting them. Did they still have a chance or were they out of the tournament?

As was customary, the coaches began practice by discussing the positive aspects of the game. The discussion took a little longer than after the Morgan game, thanks to an excellent fourth quarter. This was comforting for the team, but they had a question that had to be answered. Finally one of the players asked, "Do we still have a chance to make the state tournament?"

Coach wrote something with his blue marker on a diagram board. Without saying a word, he turned the board around so the team could read, "0-0."

The team was still interpreting what the message meant when Coach smiled at them and broke the silence, "The past is behind us and we haven't lost too many games to prevent us from winning the state championship this year."

"If we ever lose too many games, will you tell us as soon as possible?" begged a voice from the group.

"I promise you will be the first to know," answered Coach.

The boys cheered as they rushed onto the court to prepare for a game the next day, Friday, at home against another good team with an identical season record at 8-7. The rival, Bear River Bears would be in town to take a bite out of the Buffs, but the herd was ready for their attack. The attitude of the Buffaloes had been pumped up with a dose of motivation. The agony of defeat is often heart rendering but the agony of failing to allow destiny to continue its course would be an indescribable pain. Pain had been avoided and a determined group of boys and coaches were still on the right path.

Nick Drake, a sports editor, described the game with his normal, accurate, heart-pumping, and love-for-the-game enthusiasm. "Tooele Coach Gary Alverson knows his team is in a tight race for a state playoff berth in a very even region.

"And the veteran Buff mentor also knows that for a squad to have a chance to fight for post season play, home victories are a must to stay in the hunt. But after three quarters the score was in favor of the Bears at 36-31. All hopes of a league triumph over region rival Bear River was dimming as fast as the Tooele County fog.

"However, the Buffs picked up the defensive intensity down the stretch. The hosts finally caught fire in the fourth quarter to erase the deficit and pull out a win by outscoring the Bears in the final frame 16-5. The triumph was a hard fought vital victory that ended 47-41. Mike Holt scored eighteen points and Taylor Palmer scored eleven."

Nick Drake interviewed Coach after the game. He said, "The victory was vital for the Buffs bid to earn one of the four coveted state berths from the Region 11 ranks this winter. We played one of our most consistent games overall this year. We were able to play a good team. Our kid's intensity and our defense were very good. They made the biggest difference. Bear River turned it over quite a bit and we made our free throws in the end. Castle and Boucher made five of six down the stretch. That was a huge win for us."

The Buffs were well pleased. In the minds of the players and coaches they were right on track again. The season was moving ahead quickly and they were thrilled to have a perfect record again, one win and zero losses.

> *I don't know the key to success, but the key to failure is trying to please everybody.*
>
> *Bill Cosby*

> *Whoever said, "It's not whether you win or lose that counts, probably lost."*
>
> *Martina Navratalova*

Chapter Eleven
Unity in Action

And I wear it for another hundred thousand who have died
believen' that we all were on their side.
Man in Black—Johnny Cash

A rare break in the schedule gave the Buffs seven full days before the next game. This extended time off allowed more practices and more time to prepare for the future. The coaches had been keeping a list so there would be plenty to cover but there was also time to regroup for a breath of fresh air. During a practice, Coach singled out the first player to return to the court after a water break. He complimented the player for putting extra effort into practice drills and even mentioned the boy was doing much better in his school work. The player felt uplifted that Coach had recognized his improvements and hoped the conversation would continue. He noticed Coach was wearing the same yellow rubber bracelet during the week of practice that he had worn at the last game so he inquired, "What is written on your yellow wrist band?"

Coach held his arm where the words "LIVESTRONG" could be read on the band.

"Why do you wear it?" asked the player who suspected the wristband had some significance.

"I wear it because I can," Coach responded. "I am still alive, still able to carry a message about the reality and urgency of cancer, finding a cure, and preventing it. I wear a yellow bracelet for the voices that can no longer be heard from friends and loved ones we can no longer see, but whose presence we can still feel."

Although Coach appeared to be as strong as ever, his comment was a sobering reminder that many lives were being held in the balance due to cancer.

On October 2, 1996, at age twenty-five, Lance Armstrong was diagnosed with stage three testicular cancer. The cancer had spread to his lungs, abdomen, and brain. His prognosis was poor. He was coughing up blood and had a very painful tumor. Immediate surgery and chemotherapy were required to save his life. His diseased testicle and his brain tumors were removed and found to contain extensive dead tissue (necrosis). After his surgeries his doctors admitted that he had less than a forty percent chance of survival.

Lance went through chemotherapy treatments that consisted of a cocktail containing at least five drugs. His last treatment was on December 13, 1996. His cancer surprisingly went into remission then with perseverance and long suffering he built his body and attitude into that of a world class athlete.

He won the Tour de France a record-breaking seven consecutive years, 1999-2005, to become the world's premiere cyclist of all time. He is the only person to win seven times, having broken the previous record of five wins.

In 1999, he was named the American Broadcasting Company (ABC) Wide World of Sports Athlete of the Year. In 2000 he won the Prince of Asturias Award in Sports.[In 2002, *Sports Illustrated* magazine named him Sportsman of the Year. He was also named Associated Press Male Athlete of the Year for the years 2002–2005. He received ESPN's ESPY Award for Best Male Athlete in 2003, 2004, 2005, and 2006, and won the BBC Sports Personality of the Year Overseas Personality Award in 2003. Armstrong retired from racing on July 24, 2005, which was the end of the 2005 Tour de France, but returned to competitive cycling in January 2009, finishing third in the 2009 Tour de France.

Most importantly, he never forgot or ignored his fellow cancer sufferers. As his strength improved in 1997, he founded the Lance Armstrong Foundation (LAF). LAF was founded on the principle that knowledge is power, and encourages individuals to adopt the channeled, focused energy that Lance Armstrong used in his own battle with cancer. LAF steps in at the moment of diagnosis to offer pragmatic information and tools to assist cancer patients and their families through the challenging process of treatment.

Coach understood the story very well. For champion cyclist and cancer survivor Lance Armstrong, yellow is more than just the color of the jersey of the leader of the Tour de France. It's a symbol for hope, courage, and perseverance. In May of 2004 the LAF began to raise funds by selling yellow LIVESTRONG wristbands.

The comments by the head coach were relayed quickly to the rest of the team and soon there were five coaches and fifteen basketball players who proudly wore a yellow LIVESTRONG wristband. Within a few more days the students and faculty in every class were wearing the yellow LIVESTRONG wristbands not just to celebrate Armstrong's courageous battle against cancer and his inspiration to millions of people to overcome adversity, but to join a group that would eventually surpass 47.5 million people. All of them were working together to conquer cancer.

It was evident Coach was impressed by the Lance Armstrong Foundation and he was actively supporting cancer victims everywhere. Coach and every individual who wear the LIVESTRONG wristband proudly understand the strength and message of the organization. "We don't live in the same city or compete in the same events, but we're one team. What unites us are hope, courage and determination. We are more than one."

Cancer patients often experience a change in priorities and search for a new meaning in life. Coach Alverson had developed a strong faith and a sense of something greater than himself many years before. As a result of that faith, when he was between the age of nineteen and twenty-one, he served as a missionary in the Central States Mission, in North Carolina and Virginia, for the Church of Jesus Christ of Latter Day Saints. He was one of two assistant presidents, which illustrated that he was an example of hard work and dedication to his faith as a young man among many other missionaries his same age. Now that same faith was his foundation of strength and determination to cope with cancer.

No one wants to foster false hope, but hope is sometimes all a person has to get through a grueling disease. Hope is important. Hope provides strength. Fighting a disease like mesothelioma requires an incredible amount of strength. Coach was in a better position because he had faith and faith is stronger than hope.

Some people with cancer draw strength from their families, other victims of cancer, or spiritual convictions, while others take stock in their accomplishments and become determined to persevere through their struggle. In addition to these strengths Coach had his team, his assistant coaches, his students, and his community to support him. As long as hope is alive, the struggle against cancer is never in vain. With faith he was able to say, "I can win this fight; there is no type of cancer that someone has not beaten."

> *Anything is possible. You can be told that you have a 90% chance or a 50% chance or a 1% chance, but you have to believe and you have to fight."*
>
> *Lance Armstrong*

> *Pain is temporary, quitting lasts forever.*
>
> *Lance Armstrong*

> *Whether you think you can or whether you think you can't, you're right.*
>
> *Henry Ford*

Chapter Twelve
You Gotta Get Back Up

You can chase a dream that seems so out of reach and you know it
might not ever come your way. Dream it anyway
Do it Anyway--Martina McBride

The first round of the region schedule was over. The teams were scheduled to play each other twice, once on each team's home court. In reality, the Buffaloes were three wins and two losses in region play. The Buffs would play an away game with the Ogden Tigers to start the second round on Friday, January 28, 2005.

At different times during the year, basketball coaches nationwide participate in a variety of local and national events to raise funds and awareness for Coaches vs. Cancer. The coaches from Tooele have participated in an event that was started in 1993, known as "Suits and Sneakers." Every year "Suits and Sneakers," a national event designed to raise awareness about Coaches vs. Cancer and the importance of cancer prevention with early detection, is promoted by the National Association of Basketball Coaches and the American Cancer Society.

During the designated weekend, coaches and coaching staffs nationwide wear sneakers with their suits while coaching games to remind basketball audiences about the many ways people can reduce their risk of cancer, like eating right, exercising, making healthy lifestyle choices, and following the American Cancer Society's recommended cancer screening guidelines.

American Cancer Society researchers estimated that there were about 1,450,000 million new cancer cases and about 562,000 cancer deaths in 2005. The news was sad but some promising news was that for all cancers diagnosed from 1996-2004, the five year survival rate was sixty-six percent, up from fifty percent in 1975-1977. The increase reflected improvements in both early detection and treatment. A drop of one or two percent per year may sound small, but it adds up to 650,000 cancer deaths being avoided over fifteen years. If the rate kept dropping, it meant 100,000 people each year who may have died from cancer would live to celebrate another birthday. Coach and his assistants believed in the lifesaving progress and actively participated with thousands of supporters to make sure the fight to beat cancer continued.

The Friday game against Ogden High School was the date set for the "Suits and Sneakers" event. It was rare to see the coaches wearing sneakers on their feet with dress slacks and a tie but it was rarer to see them at a game wearing a complete suit with sneakers. The coaches took it well but as humorous as they looked, they were serious about beating cancer.

The Buffs came out strong outscoring the Tigers 23 to 10 in the first quarter before continuing to a 59 to 41 route at the final buzzer. Tooele had three players in double figures-Holt scored eighteen, Lockie ten, and Hogan ten. In the minds of the Buffaloes, the team was on track at 2-0. To the rest of the 3A League they were 4-2 in region play and 10-7 overall.

Five days later, Wednesday, February 2, the coaches wore suits and sneakers again, this time against their county archrival, the Grantsville Cowboys. In fashion with the game played three weeks earlier in Tooele, the Grantsville gymnasium was packed to capacity. It was a barn burner through the first quarter; the score was the Buffs 17 and the Cowboys 16 before the Buffs took off on a scoring binge to win the game 55 to 45. Tooele had four players in double figures- Holt scored fourteen, Boucher thirteen, Lockie ten, and Hogan ten. The Cowboys may have lost but Derek Ericksen reached into his bag of determination to display a "never give up" attitude. Using long range missiles that appeared to be guided by radar he hit a barrage of six three-point shots on his way to score twenty-five points. The Buffaloes returned home with what they believed was a perfect 3-0 record. They were where they were supposed to be. Coach looked strong and as if he could not be happier.

The practices and games were coming fast and furious but the hectic pace didn't hide the dark cloud hovering over the next game. The Morgan Trojans were coming to Tooele with the number forty-three dominating the conversations and predictions everywhere. The loss at Morgan by forty-three points was an earth shattering obstacle to overcome. The Tooele coaches attempted to eliminate the distraction in every conceivable way during the five days prior to tip off. However, the nagging pain from losing so badly three weeks earlier was not just resurrecting itself for the Buffs, it was intensifying.

The Buffs were able to play a better defensive game but on offense they were out of sync appearing to dance to the beat of five different drummers again. The Trojans held the Buffs to a measly three points in the first quarter, just six more in the second, and nine in the third quarter. The next quarter was a little brighter for the Buffs but they could only match the Trojans with thirteen points in the fourth quarter. The Buffs were thoroughly drubbed from the tip-off until the game ending buzzer finally showed them mercy. The final score Morgan 49 and Tooele 31. Morgan left town with a spotless record of 19 wins and 0 losses. In two games the Trojans had beat the Buffs by a total of sixty-one points.

Nick Drake was able to catch the Tooele coach for a postgame interview. "Defensively we were very good," Coach Alverson noted. "But offensively we struggled and were tentative in the first half. We just stood around instead of moving and the further behind we got the worse it got. Then, we weren't as patient as I would have liked."

The eighteen point loss was just as devastating to the Buffs as the forty-three point slaughter had been. The Buffs were hit with the staggering reality that they had lost three games in region action. When they met with the coaches in their locker room after the game they could not wait until practice - the agonizing weight was too heavy. A player quickly asked, "Coach, you told us you would let us know when we were out of the picture for the playoffs. Have we lost too many games?"

Three losses that included one at home seriously complicated the situation but this was an interest Coach understood better than anyone. He knew the records of every team in Region 11. He knew what games remained to be played by every team. He understood the selection process for the state tournament and how each team would fit into the 3A Tournament schedule brackets. Every complicated variable and surprise was understood by him. The team and even the coaches were fearful of what the ever-optimistic head coach was about to say. And what would a chance mean anyway, when the Buffs needed to get past Morgan to win the state championship.

Life was becoming confusing; terrible things were being said about the future of Coach Alverson regarding his cancer; no one gave them a chance to win another game, and people wondered why they were failing the call of destiny that impressed them so forcefully. As fast as a lightning strike, the naysayers were back. Fans felt let down. The lonely basketball court during practice became the place of refuge again. One specific spot in the center of a twister, hurricane, or tornado is calm and serene in the midst of the surrounding chaos - the court was in the eye of the storm.

After thinking about the question for several seconds and allowing the team to do some pondering of their own, the coach walked silently to the whiteboard in his team's locker room. The team and coaches looked hopeful but the expression on Coach's face left them skeptical. There must be something Coach wanted to explain to them. After a few moments, he said, "There are two games left before the tournament. I will never be able to say our record is 0-0 again. We cannot lose even one game. We must play the six toughest teams that State 3A can suit up in order to win the championship. But today our record is 0-0. We have not been eliminated yet." He reached for a blue marker that was always in his shirt pocket then wrote on the whiteboard, "0-0."

Their total season record was 11-8 but the coaches and the boys were as exuberant as if they had just extended a perfect record to 19-0. With renewed energy and a positive outlook for the challenging quest, which was awaiting them, they couldn't wait to begin preparation at the next practice. The past became a building block they had climbed and they were moving forward.

> *Basketball doesn't build character, it reveals it.*
>
> *Unknown*

> *The best teams have chemistry. They communicate with each other and they sacrifice personal glory for the common goal.*
>
> *Dave DeBusscherre*

Chapter Thirteen
Gotta Go, Right Now!

*And another one gone, and another one gone, another one bites
the dust. Hey, I'm gonna get you too.*
Another One Bites the Dust--Queen

Every Wednesday at four o'clock, a siren sounds throughout Tooele
County, the dogs howl, and visitors prepare to panic. A crackling replaces
the siren then a spine chilling voice leads the howling a few decibels louder,
"This is a test, this is only a test. If this had been an emergency ..."

The team was doing some last minute preparation for the game that
night. It was Wednesday so the Tooele County Emergency alarm sounded
at its normal time. When it ended one of the players was wondering if
he heard it correctly. He attempted to repeat it in a quizzical tone, "Life
is a test. It is only a test. If this had been a real life test you would have
been instructed where to go and what to do." With his teammates they
had become a group of survivors who understood the new version of the
alarm. They had been taught well and they knew what to do. When you
are bombarded with problems, bad news, and insurmountable odds that
seem to never end, you can view them as challenges so that when you
overcome them you have passed the test.

Three losses in region games continued to plague the minds of the
Buffs who were beginning to question their call to be a team of destiny.
Without a boost from destiny they had no chance to accomplish the

difficult task of winning the state championship. The coaches did the best they could to encourage the team but the nagging memory of the losses to Morgan continued to take a toll on them. They also realized there were many more excellent teams. Another meeting to regroup as a team became inevitable.

Prior to the game they met in the locker room again. The atmosphere was calm and seriousness prevailed while several players summarized the importance of their pact and the dire situation in which they had found themselves. Coach had made an indelible mark in their conscience that they could not lose another game. This meant they must win six consecutive games against championship quality teams. They must do it. Another burning was in their heart that they could not deny. A still small voice was whispering to them: "Do your best, do not assume destiny will do it for you, but do your best to the very end without giving up, and then destiny will help you with the rest!"

Every player recommitted himself. This time they would not be denied by another great team or deterred by the constant comments from the naysayers. A code was chosen to remind them another loss would end their journey. They used indelible ink to write the code on the side of their basketball shoes, "FCA," meaning "for Coach Alverson." A "Team of Destiny" was ready to move forward but little did they know: the winning was not for Alverson; Coach was determined that winning would be for them. "We can win one," he always said.

The Buffs were pumped up to a high level but an excellent team awaited them. The Ben Lomond Scots were in Tooele with not only a 6-2 record in Region 11 but a sixteen point victory over the Buffs three weeks before. As the game progressed, the Scots were as strong as anticipated but the Buffs quickly demanded some respect that was missing in the first game. The first quarter was a defensive dream, ending 5-3 for Tooele. At the end of the half the Scots stayed with Tooele and tied the score 15-15. In the third quarter the Scots outscored the Buffs again making the score 29-26 for Ben Lomond. When the two teams met for the first game the third quarter had ended 51-26 for Ben Lomond.

The liveliest creature on the court during the first meeting turned out to be a White Buffalo. This night the same White Buffalo was at it again, dancing and swaying through the crowd: casting its charm from the edges of the court to the rafters, and successfully building excitement and encouragement for the other Buffaloes. Then just as effectively it lured the Scots and half of the students into a trance. The fans said it would have taken two of Miley Cyrus to have as many moves as one White Buffalo.

The dramatic improvement by the Buffaloes was a shock to the Scots who realized they were in a pivotal game to qualify for a tournament berth. They broke out of the trance induced by the White Buffalo to bravely fight to keep the lead during the fourth quarter but the powerful Scots broke loose to increase the lead with a seemingly insurmountable score of 39-33, with just fifty seconds left in the game.

Time-out was called by the Buffaloes but everyone in the gymnasium knew what the coaches for the Scots were saying, "Time is on our side; we have a big lead; let the air out of the ball (burn as much time off the clock as possible unless you have a perfect shot); force the Buffs to foul to stop the clock; hit your free throws, and we win by ten."

The coaches for the Buffs made a defensive adjustment. Then they reminded the players, "Just touch the ball. Touch the passes. Touch the dribbling. Get a finger on the ball but don't foul unless we tell you."

The assistant coaches made comments to encourage the team, but just before the team started back onto the court, Coach simply said, "I want you to remember one more thing for the next fifty seconds. This is it!"

The players knew what he was referring to as a feeling burned deep inside their chest. But the feeling was small compared to the blaze that replaced the burning when Coach turned around his clipboard. In big blue numbers it read, "0-0."

Taylor Palmer immediately got a finger on the ball for a steal then scored on a layup to cut the lead to four. A few seconds later, Mike Holt made a steal to score another layup to cut the score to two. The clock was working against the Buffs. The Scots would secure a victory if they ran a few remaining seconds off the clock or if they forced the Buffs to foul. But Taylor Palmer slightly tipped the ball again that led to another surprising steal; if the Buffs could beat the buzzer they could force the game into overtime. They still had a chance.

Palmer passed the ball to Holt who was racing toward the basket. Meanwhile, five Scots were racing to stop him from scoring another layup to tie the game. Holt could see no way to get to the basket but with unsurpassed basketball savvy he passed the ball back outside to the far corner. The surprised crowd moaned because the buzzer would soon sound. Cody Castle was there, he hadn't taken a shot all night, but he was wide open with just four seconds to play. Castle calmly threw up the ball that flew across the court until it dropped into the middle of the basket. The shot didn't tie the game; it was a three-point dagger that ended the game, 40-39 for the Buffaloes. In an unbelievable effort they scored seven points in the closing minute of the game after scoring just five points in the entire first quarter.

The Tooele coaches and the rest of the team ran onto the court to celebrate with the players. Then the coaches quickly gathered them up to usher them off the court and away from the herd of stampeding students. In the safety of the locker room, the team could hear the cheers from the band, cheerleaders, Sha-Ronns (pep club), students, and the ever energetic White Buffalo.

Reporter Nick Drake was on a winning streak of his own. Immediately following the game he caught the winning coach for an interview. "These kids showed tremendous character to rally in the final minute to pull out a dramatic triumph. It was a well deserved win," Coach Alverson stated. "I thought we executed the game plan. Holt made it happen with his quarterbacking. I felt like our other players took turns helping us. Lockie played a great game. I thought Castle played a good floor game and hit a big basket. Palmer coming off the injured shoulder and coming back in the last quarter played a great game and great defense. Hogan had a big put-back basket, played great defense, and got some big rebounds. Lawrence had another great game, big rebounds, and kept the ball alive. I like the way Alex Despain played and he's been working hard in practice; so hard it gets him in games.

"It was a huge win and an exciting win," he added. "I thought our total team defense was great. Now we have a chance to control our own destiny to tie for second place in Region 11. We have to help ourselves by beating Bear River."

The next day at school the importance of the win was sinking into the minds of the students as word spread rapidly throughout the student body. The final season game was at Bear River the following night, February 11. The students began to feel the excitement of an additional game in tournament action. Coach felt the importance of the game with the Bear River Bears in ways the team and students didn't even consider.

It has been said that a professional pays attention to the detail amateurs don't even think about. Coach was a true professional who understood the ins and outs of every possibility and every advantage that would exist when the teams were assigned a line on the chart for the tournament brackets. To get the best assignment possible he needed two things. The first was a win against a very good Bear River team on their home court and the second would occur at some point right after the game. But first things first: beating the Bears was of paramount importance for his team.

Always listen to the experts. They'll tell you what can't be done and why. Then do it.

Robert Heinlein

The journey is the reward.

Chinese proverb

Chapter Fourteen
Backs Against the Wall

But when you're blinded by your pain a small, but still, resilient
voice says help is very near.
When You Believe—David Archeleta

Back at school, Coach looked like he always did which lightened the concern and fear the students had about his health. They were wary of his situation just the same. In an English class the students were assigned to research a story to use as an inspirational essay. At least thirty essays were submitted to the teacher. More than twenty-five directly alluded to the basketball coach but not one mentioned his name. An unwritten and unspoken code persuaded the students not to mention the coach with even the slightest potential negative outcome. To avoid a curse, bad luck, or perhaps a look of ignorance the students mentioned different names and slightly different situations. It did happen but very rarely was the coach mentioned by name in any class.

Excellent research produced much better essays than expected by the teacher. The student's identity was taken from all of the essays then posted on the wall for everyone to read. A few days later the teacher gave each student a small piece of paper. She instructed the students to write the title of two essays that were the most inspiring to them. Then in an anonymous fashion, they were to deposit the paper in a ballot box on her desk.

The next day she reported the outcome. A boy and a girl volunteered to read the essays that had won the balloting, neither essay was new to the teacher but she loved them both. The first one read was the longer of the two. The boy had a strong voice that could be heard all over the classroom. He read the following story.

Put Me In Coach

A teenager lived alone with his father, and the two of them had a very special relationship. Even though the son was always on the bench, his father was always in the bleachers cheering. He never missed a game. This young man was the smallest of the class when he entered high school. But his father continued to encourage him but also made it very clear that he did not have to play basketball if he didn't want to.

But the young man loved basketball and decided to hang in there. He was determined to try his best at every practice, and perhaps he'd get to play when he became a senior. All through high school he never missed a practice or a game, but remained a bench warmer all four years. His faithful father was always in the bleachers. Even though his son did not play you could occasionally hear him shout words of encouragement for his son.

Sometimes the faces in the crowd would turn to look at him then turn to the bench to look at his son who never played. The father always had a smile and appeared to be enthusiastic about the game. When his father's words of encouragement reached his ears above the crowd, the boy would always stop watching the game to turn around and give his father a smile and wink of his eye.

When the young man went to the state university, he decided to try out for the basketball team as a "walk-on." Everyone was sure he could never make the cut, but he did. The coach admitted that he kept him on the roster because he always put his heart and soul into every practice, and at the same time, provided the other members with the spirit and hustle they badly needed. He had a perfect attitude about life that was uplifting to the coach. The news that he had survived the cut thrilled him so much that he rushed to the nearest phone and called his father. His father shared his excitement so the boy arranged a way with his coach to get season tickets for all the college games. He proudly rushed them to his dad.

His father always found the time and a way to travel several miles to get to every game at a big university his son attended. Then, just like he did when his son sat on the bench in high school, he occasionally shouted words of encouragement to his son. The faces in the crowd would look at him then turn to his son. His son would smile and wink back at his dad and it was obvious that both were filled with enthusiasm just to be together at the game.

This persistent young athlete never missed practice during his four years at the state university, but he never had an opportunity to play a single minute. It was the end of his senior basketball season, and as he trotted onto the court at a practice shortly before the final game, the coach met him with a telegram. The young man opened the envelope, read the telegram, and he became deathly silent. Swallowing hard, he mumbled to the coach, "My father died this morning. Is it all right if I miss practice today?" The coach put his arm gently around his shoulder and said, "This is our last week anyway so you may take it off, son. And don't worry about us or about coming back to the championship game on Friday night, we will be okay.

Friday night arrived, and the game was not going well. In the third quarter, when the team was ten points behind, a silent young man quietly slipped into the empty locker room and put on his basketball jersey. As he ran into the gymnasium, the coach and his players were astounded to see their faithful teammate return so soon after his father's death."Coach, please let me play. I've just got to play tonight," said the young man. The coach pretended not to hear him. There was no way he wanted his worst player in this close championship game. But the young man persisted, and finally feeling sorry for the kid, the coach gave in. "All right," he said."You can go in."

Before long, the coach, the players and everyone in the stands could not believe their eyes. This little unknown, who had never played before was doing everything right. The opposing team could not stop him. He ran, he passed, he blocked out, he made some steals, and he shot like a star. His team began to catch up. Soon the score was tied. In the closing seconds of the game, this kid stole the ball and drove through five opposing players all the way to the basket for the winning layup.

The fans broke loose.

The fans broke loose. His teammates hoisted him onto their shoulders. Such cheering you've never heard! Finally, after the bleachers had emptied and the team had showered and left the locker room, the coach noticed that the young man was sitting quietly in the corner all alone. He had a great big smile and his eye kept winking. The coach walked over to him, patted him on the back, and said, "Kid, I can't believe it. You were fantastic! Tell me what got into you? How did you do it?"

The young man looked at the coach, with tears forming rapidly in his eyes, and said, "Well, you knew my dad died, but did you know that my dad was blind?" The young man swallowed hard and forced another smile, "Dad came to all my games, but today was the first time he could see me play."

There wasn't a dry eye in the English classroom, a few sobbing sounds were breaking the silence, and no one was looking at anyone else. After a few moments the teacher motioned for a Polynesian girl named Rylee to come to the front to read the next research essay. Rylee's voice penetrated the room as she read the following paper.

My Sister

This is a story about a little girl named Sarah who was suffering from a terrible disease and needed blood from her five-year-old brother, who had miraculously survived the same disease. When he was suffering he developed the antibodies needed to combat the illness which made it possible for him to stay alive. The doctor explained the situation to her little brother. He said the little body of his sister, Sarah, was unable to produce the same antibodies and with no antibodies she would surely die very soon. The young boy listened attentively so the doctor asked the boy if he would be willing to give his blood to his little sister. He hesitated for only a second before taking a deep breath and saying,

"Yes doctor, I will do it if it will save Sarah. Please hurry!"

As the transfusion progressed, he lay on the bed next to his sister and suddenly smiled, as everyone did, when he saw the color returning to his sister's cheeks. Then his face grew pale, his smile faded, and tears ran down the little boy's cheek. He looked up at the doctor and asked with a trembling voice, "Will I start to die right away?" Being young, the boy had misunderstood the doctor; he thought he was going to have to give his little sister all of his blood!

The classroom was as quiet as before with the same occasional sobs and no one was looking at another person for a few minutes. Reading two stories, from among thirty that had been found by the students, was all that was needed to meet the objectives of the lesson.

Everyone's enthusiasm was elevated a few notches, in fact three students; Danny Wihongi, Blake Olsen, and Kyle McKendrick were so caught up in the basketball frenzy they made a commitment to be the Tooele High School basketball team's most energetic supporters.

After the exhausting and highly emotional thriller with Ben Lomond on Wednesday night, a Thursday practice, a day filled with classes on Friday, and a trip to Bear River High School seemed like they were playing a double header when the Buffs entered the court for warm ups. The Bears were already doing a layup drill and the Bear fans were chanting loud *grrrrs* to spur the Bears on.

As usual another unexpected surprise was waiting for the Buffs; at the edge of the court next to the visitor's bench was one lone Polynesian girl. But this surprise was a good one. She was bravely shouting a chant back across the court at her opponents and waving a handmade poster that read "Grrrr in Bear means Ouch."

The local squad knew it couldn't afford to slip up and lose either game against Ben Lomond or Bear River if it wanted the coveted second seed and home playoff game in the inter-region round of the Class 3A State Boys Basketball Tournament. They had pulled off one miracle at Ben Lomond and they were moving forward. Destiny was calling them.

As they lined up for the opening tip off, the "Team of Destiny" knew it needed to fight hard to triumph over region rival Bear River in hostile territory to have a chance to capture the runner-up seed from Region 11 ranks and a home playoff game. But the road was rough. Soon the Buffs were trailing 50-44 on the Bears' hardwoods with only a minute remaining in regulation, the situation looked pretty bleak for the boys from Tooele.

However, Mike Holt buried two clutch, pressure packed 3-point missiles, including one with six seconds left, down the stretch to force overtime and give Tooele another chance to hand their league nemesis a devastating setback at home.

In overtime Nash Lockie took over with two crucial baskets while Holt, Josh Boucher and Bryton Lawrence contributed two points each to help the Buffs outscore the Bears 10-7 to pull out another miraculous win on the road, 59-52. Danny Wihongi was on the court almost before the final buzzer to celebrate. He was followed closely by an excited White Buffalo, and the Tooele cheerleaders. Meanwhile more than five hundred fans from Bear River stood frozen in agonized silence.

Lockie stepped up to lead the scoring with twenty points. Holt poured in nineteen, Colton Hogan scored eight, Boucher had five, Lawrence had four and Taylor Palmer had four points in a heroic team effort.

In forty-eight hours the Buffs had pulled off two seemingly impossible come from behind victories against higher rated and very talented adversaries. In both wins the Buffs were six points behind with less than a minute in the game. The Buffs never gave up and they played their best right up to the final buzzer. The Buffs coach had told the team during one of the last timeouts during regulation to play hard and work hard until the end and the reward will come.

Coach needed two things to get positioned where he wanted to be in the brackets of the state tournament. The stunning victory over Bear River had blessed him with the first step now he needed the second. The Buffs were never expected to accomplish much; in fact they were predicted to finish fifth out of just six teams in Region 11. Against staggering odds they had finished Region 11 games tied with Ben Lomond for second place.

The second step looked a lot easier for the ever-optimistic coach; the Buffs had a fifty-fifty chance to win which seemed like the odds were overwhelmingly in their favor. There was no pressure on the players. This time it was up to Coach to win.

Ogden, Utah, is between Bear River and Tooele. Ben Lomond High School is in Ogden. One hour after the Tooele-Bear River game ended, a van filled with beaming coaches and an exuberant team parked at Ben Lomond High and hurried into the gym. The two opposing coaches met to determine who would be the only team in second place so they could be listed in the proper tournament bracket. The designated weapon of combat was a coin.

The strong leader of the Scots tossed the coin into the air and the brave bull from the Buffaloes yelled "heads" as the coin struck the floor. The coin bounced twice then spun on its edge. The two combatants and their thirty gladiators crowded closer to look down on the spinning coin. For a few spins "tails" could be seen then for a few spins "heads" was seen. The spinning coin appeared to have energy of its own. After what seemed like a lifetime the coin started to tip as it began to level out. "Tails" began to appear, shouts of joy were about to explode from the Scots when suddenly the coin flipped over to bang around in circles showing "heads." The momentum switched to Tooele as the coin shook in dying quivers never to roll over again, on "heads." The Buffs were ready to rumble!

It was a devastating defeat for Ben Lomond. They had spent the whole season flying high until the Buffs came to their home court in Ogden and took it away as fast as thunder starts a stampede. They had stomped the Buffs in the first game but a three point dagger at the buzzer forced the battle with a coin toss. The mysterious coin was just as deadly as the dagger. Twenty seconds was all it took for a long shot and the flip of a coin to do a hundred points worth of damage to the Scots. They would continue to play with every effort they could muster but the last haunting jump of the coin from "tails" to "heads" forced the Scots to play an away game in a very tough tournament bracket against a perennial powerhouse, Judge Memorial High School.

f anyone was converted to believe in destiny; it was the Ben Lomond s. The last six seconds on the court and a few seconds with the faloes for a coin toss inflicted painful wounds that were convincing: herd from Tooele was indeed "A Team of Destiny."

The blessings the energetic coin provided to Tooele were monumental: The Buffs would play Granite, a tough team - but tougher teams were out there - they would get to play on their home court in Tooele, and they would be placed right where Coach wanted to be in the tournament brackets. Now that the upsets and statistics were recorded in the history books to end the season in Region 11, Coach could not ask for anything better. The past was behind him and it was time to move forward into a world of unlimited surprises and innumerable possibilities.

> *I tell kids to pursue their basketball dreams, but I tell them to not let that be their only dream.*
>
> Kareem Abdul Jabbar

> *You are never really playing an opponent. You are playing yourself, your own highest standards, and when you reach your limits. That is real joy.*
>
> Arthur Ashe

Chapter Fifteen
One More Game?

When it's over so they say, it'll rain on a sunny day. I wanna know: have you ever seen the rain comin' down on a sunny day?
Have You Ever Seen The Rain—Creedence Clearwater Revival

As soon as Coach returned to Tooele, the vigilant Nick Drake caught him again, "It was a big win at Bear River. I don't know how long it has been since we've beat them up there," said the coach. "Then we won the coin toss. I called heads and we won it.

"It has been a while since we had a home court game going into the state tournament. The kids earned everything. We were picked to finish fifth but the kids really worked hard and earned the seven wins we got in a tough league. Granite is a good team. They won twelve games and finished third in their league. They have two great scorers in Williams, averaging seventeen point five points per game, and Waddoups, who has a fourteen point five average. They are a good team so we have to play our best ball and take advantage of the opportunity we have playing on our home court. We need to go into the rest of the playoffs on a winning note and on a roll. We're feeling good about ourselves," smiled Coach.

Mesothelioma remained a hot subject in the classrooms at THS. It was learned that a well known actor had experienced the same cancer. Twenty-five years before, malignant mesothelioma took the life of Hollywood legend Steve McQueen. McQueen is remembered for his roles in such movie classics as: *The Great Escape, Sand Pebbles, Bullitt, The Getaway,* and *Papillon*. What few people realize is that the superstar's life was cut short at the age of fifty by the disease.

McQueen had been surrounded by asbestos all of his life. As a young adult, Thirty years earlier McQueen served as a Marine. He worked construction jobs at shipyards where he was responsible for stripping asbestos off the pipes used in naval ships. He was an avid car racer and may have been exposed to asbestos when repairing the brake linings of race cars. The protective helmets and driving suits he wore also contained asbestos. The association with asbestos filled every exciting adventure of his young life.

Suddenly a surprising discovery catapulted him into a battle for his life. He developed a routine cough in 1978. The cough gradually worsened until he had difficulty breathing on a movie set the following year. McQueen barely ran fifteen yards during the filming of an action sequence before requesting oxygen assistance. Later in 1979, doctors diagnosed him with mesothelioma. An incurable cancer related to asbestos exposure had attacked the lining of his lungs and had already done irreparable damage.

The chief of oncology at a prominent hospital in Los Angeles told McQueen that he was suffering from a high-grade malignancy of mesothelioma. He was told that such a cancer would be virulent, spreading from his lungs to other organs throughout his body. The oncologist did not know of a patient who had been cured of mesothelioma. In desperation, McQueen's doctor treated him with radiation therapy to try to shrink the tumor.

Frustrated by the failing treatments, McQueen switched to a controversial treatment regimen to cure the cancer that had spread to his pancreas. The treatment was based on the notion that cancers grew from a lack of enough pancreatic enzymes.

At the time he was diagnosed in 1979, McQueen's doctors told him that there was no cure for malignant mesothelioma. They ruled against chemotherapy and surgery as treatment options, leaving McQueen with no choice but to seek out alternative treatments. In July of 1980, McQueen traveled to Rosarita Beach, Mexico, to be treated in a cancer clinic. He underwent a torturous three-month regimen that involved fetal animal injections, laetrile treatments (a controversial drug made from apricot pits), ingesting more than 100 vitamins per day, coffee enemas, massages, and spiritual sessions.

In October of 1980, McQueen felt encouraged by the improvement of his condition. He publicly thanked Mexico for showing the world a new alternative to treat cancer and for saving his life.

McQueen's resurgence was short-lived. Less than one month later, in November of 1980, doctors operated to remove cancerous masses from McQueen's abdomen and neck. McQueen survived the surgery, but he died the next day, his body was riddled with cancer.

Whenever a fact or story was learned about cancer it was shared in many ways among the faculty and students. Some of them were surprised but everyone was happy and encouraged that the coach kept looking strong.

During the months that Coach was treated for pleural-mesothelioma another movie star named Paul Gleason was undergoing treatment for the same cancer. Best known for his performances in movies like *The Breakfast Club, Trading Places* and *Van Wilder*, Paul Gleason was more than just an actor; he was an athlete, poet, husband, and father.

Before Mr. Gleason decided to pursue a career on the big screen, he had aspirations of becoming a major league baseball star. He starred for years in the minor leagues before happening upon the film that would change the course of his life: 1961's *Splendour in the Grass*. It was to be the start of an illustrious forty years in Hollywood starring in all genres of film and television.

Gleason fought a long and courageous battle right up to the end against malignant pleural mesothelioma. He was severely weakened but still fighting when the rare and merciless cancer caused his death on May 29, 2006. He was sixty-seven.

On Friday, February 18, the Granite Farmers took the court in Tooele for the first round playoff game. The Buffs appeared poised and ready. The gymnasium was packed to maximum capacity reminiscent of the rivalry games against the Grantsville Cowboys. The Granite and Tooele cheerleaders were on the court with the White Buffalo and three new number one fans: Danny Wihongi, Blake Olsen, and Kyle McKendrick.

There was another popular attraction to cheer the Buffs on. A small, dark haired girl about eight years old was dressed in a Tooele cheerleading dress and waving purple and white pom-poms on the court to excite the crowd. She was probably a younger sister of one of the cheerleaders and very cute. Fifteen minutes were ticking down before tipoff and the crowd was already in a frenzy of anticipation.

The Buffs started strong with a quick basket by Lockie then Boucher added a three-point bomb. Cory Waddoups kept the Buffs from pulling away with a three point bomb of his own then Anthony Lintz and Travis Page added a basket for the Farmers before the Buffs retook the lead.

In the second quarter the Farmers caught up to tie the score again at 15-15. The Buffs took a one point lead on a free throw by Lockie but Waddoups hit another three point bomb, to make it 18-16 for the Farmers.

With 4:38 left in the first half Castle made a steal, then a pass to Holt who made a pass to Lockie for a layup to tie the score at 18-18, and the half ended 20-20. Hogan opened the third quarter with a layup but the Farmers ran up the next six points to lead 26-22. Lockie scored the next three points, and it was 26-25.

The lead went back and forth until the closing moments of the third period with the Buffs trailing by two; Lockie grabbed an offensive rebound then tossed the ball to the outside to Castle. He was on his favorite part of the floor in the far corner in the exact place he had thrown the dagger that buried Ben Lomond at the buzzer. He tossed the ball again; another dagger, a three-point shot to put the Buffs back in the lead 41-40. Cory Waddoups and Keith Williams, big time "money players," for the Farmers, kept the game close enough that they could have pulled off a win on the slightest miscue by the Buffs, but after Castle's dagger to take the lead the Farmers never led again. When the final buzzer sounded the score was Tooele 55 and Granite 50.

The bleachers emptied onto the court while the Tooele coaches rounded up the players to usher them to the locker room.

The Buffs game plan was to play as a team against two of the top money players in the tournament. Sports writer Nick Drake characterized the effort, "When it counted, the Buffs' philosophy proved to be true; the sum of a complete team is greater than or equal to a squad with a pair of strong players. The THS team parlayed key offensive and defensive contributions from five different players down the stretch to pull away from the determined Farmers and register a hard fought playoff victory."

The Buffs had a balanced team effort with steals, assists, rebounds, defense, and hustle. The scoring was Holt eight points, Boucher eight, Lockie seventeen, Hogan ten, Palmer seven, and Castle five.

The team picked to finish fifth in a six team region moved forward to be among just eight teams that remained in the state tournament. The Buff' fans and students were wound up with excitement that the Buffs would get to play one more game.

> *My responsibility is getting all my players playing for the name on the front of the jersey, not the one on the back.*
> *Unknown*

> *Good, better, best. Never let it rest. Until your good is better and your better is best.*
> *Tim Duncan*

Chapter Sixteen
In Coach's Territory

In the warrior's code, there's no surrender. Though his body says stop, his spirit cries never.

Burnin' Heart--Survivor

Coach was in the position he had hoped for all season with a chance to play a good team in the tournament bracket. The Dixie Flyers had become the first team in three years to post a 3A victory on the road by upsetting highly favored Emery 54-51 in Castledale. Although Dixie was a good team the Tooele coach was happy to avoid a showdown with Emery.

"Now we play a big team," Coach noted. "They are the only team to win a 3A tournament game on the road in three years. That is a big win for them. We have to strap it up and see if we can get the next game. They have two very good wing players, averaging fourteen points per game and they are very athletic. They have some good senior players that are very physical.

"We have to keep them in a half court game and make it very difficult for them to score and get in rhythm. It should be fun. We're looking forward to it. We're hoping we can play our best ball. Now we just have to get ready. I've stressed to the players that we need to take advantage of this opportunity. This scenario doesn't happen every year, so I told them to take advantage of it and enjoy it."

The Buffs were fighting the same insurmountable odds as always. The fans were excited the team would play one more game. The Coach was where he wanted to be but one more game was not enough. Expecting to play only one more game would be like giving up. The championship game was the one that counted when he repeated again, "We can win one!"

During the week before the next game Coach was scheduled for a chemotherapy treatment. In preparation he had to take seven pills during the twenty-four to forty-eight hours prior to the treatment to control nausea. The pills were just some of many that were prescribed for him. After the insurance paid their share, each one of the seven pills still cost $100.

At this point the treatments were at least six hours long and very exhausting. Eventually the treatments were shortened to four hours and performed every three weeks. After each treatment Coach surprisingly made the forty mile trip to attend the practice session at 2:30. He was determined to beat the cancer and to convince the individuals on his team to be the very best they could be. No one but Coach and his players gave the Buffs a reasonable chance to win a state championship. It was impossible, they whined, but Coach said, "We can win one!" The doctors told him the same bleak things but he had an answer for them too, "I can beat this!"

The boys knew they were a "Team of Destiny" because they could feel it, they could hear it whispering to them, and they witnessed the unimaginable events that transpired time after time to provide just enough boost to keep them moving forward. They had lost some close games when they hadn't done the best they could to deserve the help of destiny but they learned from those games to become better. They also realized that when they had played the best they had ever played, but were still falling short down the wire, that destiny had stepped in at the last moment to save them.

At first they expected destiny to make them winners by a comfortable margin and put very little pressure on them. Eventually they recognized they had to do their best right up to the end then destiny would keep them close before pushing them ahead. There were times they doubted destiny but the forgiving persistence of it was always there with just enough help to keep them moving forward. The miracles were so frequent and obvious they could not be misunderstood.

Many sports writers and announcers describe a team as Cinderella, underdog, destiny, David against Goliath, or a dark horse running against the odds. A "Team of Destiny" is more. Destiny may be envisioned as cooperation with the Divine, or pushing the exertions of human will to a level that deserves divine intervention in response to a worthy cause of high magnitude.

It isn't destiny for a great player to win or when a team simply surprises someone to win one miracle game. A team that suddenly wins against the odds is not a team of destiny, which is why the game is played on the court by the players instead of on paper by the experts. The Cinderella team is not a team of destiny because they play with surprising intensity to succeed in a tournament. A true "Team of Destiny" has setbacks but continues to fight against the odds with all they have right up to the end, they never give up, and they inspire others to do better each day for a greater cause than athletic achievement. They earn the blessings of destiny.

The Buffaloes had a serious cause - cancer had hit their coach hard. They were doing their best, sometimes better. After all they could do - remarkable events occurred. Many people were effected; at school, in the community, and throughout the world of sports and medicine. Probably most importantly, they were placed on earth to experience difficulties in order to better appreciate the good things in life and to use difficulty to make them stronger. Each one of them could learn from other people's pain and in Coach's case thousands of people were learning. These are reactions that deserve blessings and Divine intervention. These are the ingredients of a divinely inspired destiny. A destiny of this nature is not limited to sports but it occurs in many situations and professions to bless and inspire individuals and families to endure to the end as caring and compassionate examples of what we were meant to be.

The naysayers were a persistent bunch and it was an unexpected occurrence when someone was found who expected the Buffs to play more than one more game. At least they were complimentary when they spoke about the team being lucky enough to get into the tournament and even win a game. No one expected more.

The Herd was forming into a small group of edgy buffalo that were ready for another game. The win against Granite qualified Tooele to play Dixie at 2:30 on Thursday in the Class 3A State Boys Tournament. The trail was scheduled to end at the E Center in West Valley City with the championship game on Saturday.

In an interview a week before the game, Coach issued a fair warning to the Dixie coach to prepare for a ball controlled half-court game. At practice during the week the Buffs practiced exactly that. The coaches emphasized patience and defense to control the tempo of the game. They could not afford to allow the opponent to have a high number of possessions because the coaches knew the Buffs would not be able to keep up in a high scoring game.

The plan was to take the opponent out of their game, to frustrate them, and force them to rush a limited number of scoring opportunities. "Pass and move. Pass and cut. Force their defense out to you and pass," the coaches instructed. "You must be patient, use up the clock, protect the ball, and wait for a perfect shot in order for our game plan to work."

Many teams practice and expect to follow the same game plan but it rapidly falls to pieces due to impatience and becoming anxious to speed up the game. Then it comes back to haunt them. They are undisciplined and soon fall so far behind they cannot catch up to the stronger team. Coach knew from the beginning of the season that his team would listen and do exactly what he asked them to do. They would not question and they would not doubt. Once again, he would rely on what the boys knew that their mothers knew to be of value and the many important lessons their mothers had taught them. One of the most important was obedience.

> *Only those who can see the invisible, can accomplish the impossible.*
>
> *Patrick Snow,*
> *Author of "Creating Your Own Destiny"*

> *Imagination is more important than knowledge.*
> *Albert Einstein*

Chapter Seventeen
Let the Air Out

I've been up & down & over & out but I know one thing; each time I find myself flat on this face I pick myself up & get back in the race.

That's Life—Michael Buble'

Tooele High School made buses available for the students to travel the thirty-five miles to the E Center so school was let out at 12:00 noon. The students loved any excuse to miss school and the players became heroes for pulling off another game to make it possible. The team was confident they could do more, but few students believed it was possible to beat Dixie to earn another game in the state semi-finals. It was more difficult to believe that Tooele would be in the tournament with the three powerhouse teams that were still competing to be crowned the 2005 State Champions. Dixie was an excellent team and their thrashing of Region 8 Champion the week before at Emery High School in Castledale testified of their strength.

The game was videotaped by Comcast and the announcers were from Utah Sports Network. They were surprised the Buffs were still playing and knew very little about them. This confusion caused them to get started on the wrong foot by mixing up the name of the coach with the name of the principal of the school. Instead of Coach Alverson they said Coach Westover.

The herd was excited but calmly suspicious in the unfamiliar territory of state tournament competition. There weren't many fans that had attended the Buffs' great run to play and lose the championship game in 1993. Very few students knew the Buffs' won the state consolation bracket in 1970, seventeen years before any of them were born. Before that it was more obscure:, none of the students' parents could remember that the Buffs won Region in 1953.

The announcers and sports reporters were surprised the Buffs had not been eliminated but the tournament was relatively young and this round would certainly separate the wheat from the chaff. Even the Tooele cheerleaders were caught in disbelief and doubted what the basketball team would accomplish so they had gone to a national cheerleading competition in Florida. Six months earlier they had booked flights, made hotel reservations, and this week they had left Utah. No one had heard of a team playing in the state tournament without any cheerleaders before but who would have guessed the Buffs would be one of the final eight teams in 2005. One could count on their fingers the number of times they had made it to the state tournament in their ninety-two year history.

A small portion of the herd had grouped together as several hundred loyal students and alumni were watching from the bleachers. Ms. Syra and the Tooele High School Band, which consisted of at least eighty members, were ready for the game. They electrified the air with battle hymns and music that stirred the emotions of the crowd; the White Buffalo was leading cheers on the edge of the court; Blake Olsen, and Kyle McKendrick were working the crowd with big smiles; Danny Wihongi was waving his left arm, and holding up a sign with his right hand. On one side it read, "And all the Buffs were cheering." On the reverse side it read, "The Night We Drove Old Dixie Down."

A girl about eight years old with two pigtails was dressed in her purple and white cheerleader dress. She stood all alone in the center of the court, like an angel with pom-poms for wings, waving at the Tooele side of the court after each player was introduced to start the game.

Tooele's Lawrence tipped the ball to Lockie to start the game - eight minutes per quarter - and then Lockie passed to Holt at midcourt. The Buffs passed then passed again with either extreme patience or due to a good defensive effort by the Dixie Flyers. Thirty passes were made before

Boucher threw up a three pointer that missed. Dixie charged down the court but quickly committed a turnover.

The Buffs came back to the top of the key then passed and passed again. The announcers sounded bored by the slow pace of the game and talked about Dixie's drive to the playoffs and the admirable win on the road against Emery. They were very positive that Dixie was moving on in the tournament as a Cinderella team who was superior to Tooele.

At one point an announcer moaned, "That is over thirty passes by the Buffs. They are following a script straight out of the *Hoosiers* movie that would make Gene Hackman proud!" On the next possession they threw twenty-three passes before Dixie committed a foul. The announcer added, "Gene Hackman could coach this team, pass twenty-five times before you shoot." On the inbound pass Lawrence scored on a layup and was fouled in the act of shooting. He missed the free throw but the Buffs were ahead 2-0 after nearly four minutes of play.

This time it was Dixie with the ball, a pass and another pass for fifteen passes but it was obvious the Buffs were using a very intense and excellently executed matchup zone defense. The Flyers relied on a running, high-power offense that was becoming frustrated by the Buffs' defense. They began to hurry shots and after rebounding they quickly responded by throwing up off balanced shots. As the game often goes they suffered a plague of misses that went in and back out or rolled around the hoop before falling out. The Buffs continued to slow the game down on offense and dictate the tempo of the game with their matchup zone defense. Dixie finally scored twice in the closing moments of the first quarter but Tooele led 6-4.

The tempo continued, which cooled the shooting of both teams, but Dixie appeared to suffer the most until they sprinted into the lead during the final minutes of the second quarter. The Buffs made just two of eight shots but the Flyers made just four of twelve shots that included three air balls. The Buffs had played a game in the E Center earlier in the season and the experience on a bigger NBA-size court with baskets that had no walls behind them was helping them stay close to the Flyers. If they could stay close in the second half they could continue the ball control offense and the matchup zone defense. Just one foul shot was taken in the whole first half and Tooele missed it. The score was twenty to twenty-five points less for each team than what the experts expected. The low score surprised everyone but Coach. He was where he wanted to be. The Flyers led by two at the half, 12-10.

The pace was unchanged in the third quarter which continued to help the Buffs stay close. The announcers maintained the same positive outlook for the Flyers in anticipation that a scoring run would break the game wide open to force the Buffs out of their game plan. If the Buffs fell behind by more than a few baskets they would be forced to play a faster game to make up the difference. The faster game would work in favor of the Flyers who would build a bigger lead. The Buffs maintained their patience.

Both teams shot lousy for another quarter which helped the Buffs again. The Dixie Flyers had tossed up an unprecedented four air balls and the Tooele fans responded quickly with shouts of "Air ball, air ball, air ball." This added embarrassment to the poor shooting flyers. The Flyers hit three of eleven and the Buffs hit five of twelve but one was a three-pointer by Holt. Both teams ended the quarter with no free throws and surprisingly the normally hot shooting Flyers were zero for five on three-point attempts. Tooele led 21-18.

Never would anyone expect the Flyers to be held to just eighteen points in three quarters. Neither the Dixie fans nor the announcers appeared to be worried because they knew the Flyers could explode for a ten to fifteen point scoring run at any moment and they were due. With less than five minutes in the contest, Dixie couldn't change the tempo and the Buffs were obedient to the letter of the law that had been laid out by the Tooele coaches during a week of practice sessions. Coach knew they would not doubt the game plan.

If the strong Cinderella team was going to beat the Buffs they better find the glass slipper soon. Most of the calls were going Tooele's way. There was one call that was especially controversial that would have meant a five point swing in favor of the Flyers and given them a three point lead. But the call surprised every Flyers' fan and most of the Buffs' fans when the referee made his decision in favor of Tooele.

The clock was moving into Coach's corner and it would soon strike midnight for the capable Cinderella team from Dixie. The Buffs led by four then two; back and forth. Up by two Hogan made another one of his famous no-look passes, this time to Lockie for a basket. During the quarter the Buffs made a dismal five out of twelve foul shots but the Flyers made just three out of six.

The Flyers were fighting frantically to change the momentum pumped up by the Buffs as the noise grew louder and then louder. The Tooele Band began to play a song to signal that the finish line was in sight just when it dawned on the fans that the Buffs were actually going to win. There would be one more game. Tooele was ahead when the final second went to zero on the clock, 33-29. The Dixie Flyers had been grounded with a measly twenty-nine points. No one could hear the final buzzer amid the noise for a few seconds then suddenly the E Center went almost quiet.

Both teams calmly lined up to pass by each other to exchange congratulations after the game. The Dixie players appeared emotionless. Everyone in the E Center was stunned for a moment as if someone had made an unbelievable come from behind basket at the buzzer. The Flyer fans were frozen in disbelief. It took a couple of seconds for the win to register in the minds of the Tooele fans. Meanwhile, the coaches hurried the team to the locker room. They disappeared down the hallway just in time to avoid the rush from the students, fans, band members, the White Buffalo, the Sha-Ronns, and the Buffs' lone cheerleader with the two pigtails. She was waving her pom-poms to the crowd from atop of some bald headed guy's shoulders.

In the end, the talented Dixie Flyers were three hundred miles from their home in St. George, with no place else to go. One good thing was they were leaving the cold northern Utah climate to go home where the weather was nice and warm. In fact, if the Dixie Flyers were looking for warmth anywhere in Utah the only place they would find it was in St. George. Regardless of what the announcers had said during the game, the Flyers were the chosen team the experts expected to win and it was a surprising disappointment to lose to the Buffs. The Flyers were stunned and emotionless after the game. The Buffs were moving forward, way beyond expectations.

During the long trip home the team from St. George could empathize with the Egyptians when they stood in terror and wonder to witness Moses use divine intervention to cause the Red Sea to roar as it split apart to expose dry land. There was just one explanation to believe and they had become believers: the Tooele High School White Buffaloes were a "Team of Destiny."

The Flyers were facing reality but the Buffs were in a land they had roamed just once, many moons before. They did not realize the importance of the victory but Coach understood the epic event perfectly. As expected, there would be three teams in the semi-finals that put fear into the rest of 3A basketball: Snow Canyon, Wasatch, and Morgan. No one could believe Tooele was the fourth team because they had more losses during the season than the other three teams put together. They had just won one of the biggest games in school history so even the naysayers had to admit the Buffs were in the final four.

Winning the coin toss was a big break that put the Buffs in a different bracket than Morgan and Wasatch so they were scheduled to play Snow Canyon. Surely Snow Canyon would play for the championship against the winner of the Wasatch and Morgan game but that semi-final's battle was already being touted as the real championship game.

The herd continued to grow larger, it was restless, and it was moving forward with a recklessness that refused to be deterred. They were surrounded by a world of naysayers, sports writers, and teams stocked with "money players" that couldn't care less about the sound of hoof beats. The next night the games being played on paper and the predicted odds would be thrown out the window. The experts and odds makers would sit in the bleachers to watch two semi-final games. There was one point everyone agreed on that could not be disputed: the teams would gather on the court to determine the winners.

"The herd was hoping that one more miracle would happen to win just one more game but Coach was more convinced than ever. "We can win one," he said. That is just the way he was!

We have a great bunch of outside shooters. Unfortunately, all our games are played indoors.

Weldon Drew

Basketball is like photography, if you don't focus, all you have is the negative.

Dan Frisby

Chapter Eighteen
With Broken Wings

Listen and learn along the way. Just believe in yourself and
hear this voice from deep inside, it's the call of destiny.
Send Me An Angel--Scorpions

When the Buffs took the court for the second game in the semi-final round there were just three teams remaining. In the earlier game Wasatch had beaten Morgan to win the thrilling battle of the titans. Statewide, the game was promoted as the real 3A Championship Game for 2005. Snow Canyon was considered an excellent team with a powerful "money player" who had scored twenty-five points to help knock the perennial powerhouse, Judge Memorial, out of the tournament. Regardless, they were not expected to overcome either Morgan or Wasatch in the championship game. Snow Canyon's record was a stellar 20 wins with just 2 losses. Tooele was considered to be twenty to one underdogs who never mentioned their record of 15 wins and 8 losses.

Many experts described Tooele as an embarrassment to 3A basketball by even being in the tournament, not to mention the semi-finals. With eight losses and no "money player," how could anyone blame them? They expected the Snow Canyon Warriors to beat Tooele by a greater margin than they had earlier in the year at the Coal Country Classic in Castledale, Utah. The Warriors had gained strength with every game since then. At that game Snow Canyon beat the Buffs by twelve points.

Coby Leavitt scored seventeen points in the game. He was a highly rated "money player" who had recently agreed to play for Cal-Poly the next year.

Supporters murmured sounds about destiny which intensified as the herd grew with each win while the Buffs moved to the next round of the tournament. But a very vocal majority discounted the murmurs as ridiculousness. They saw the Buffs as too young, inexperienced, and below the talent level needed to compete with the three top teams that had a combined record of 63 wins and 6 losses.

Kyle McKendrick, Danny Wihongi, and Blake Olsen joined the teams warming up on the court. An energetic White Buffalo was casting its charms on the crowd to build excitement in support of the team. An eight year old girl was waving purple and white pom-poms and shouting cheers to the crowd. Adrenalin was rising to match the boldness of the band with each rallying battle hymn that they played. The Sha-Ronns, the drill team of girls from Tooele, moved along the edge of the court. There was no doubt a war was brewing in the E Center, the bleachers were shaking, a war cry was sounding, and the forces from Snow Canyon and Tooele were staring at each other eye to eye.

Teshia Haskell and Toni Cerroni were the students who dressed up as the White Buffalo. Teshia's father was sitting in the stands attempting, with difficulty due to the noise, to converse with a lady to his right. His son, Brock, was coming up through Coach's new basketball training program. Coach Dan Haskell was a lifelong athlete who was very familiar with all types of athletics, competition, the associated politics that affected teams, and the unforeseen challenges of the game. He had coached several high school teams and he understood more than the average fan. In 1998 he was the junior varsity coach at Grantsville High School when the Cowboys won the state championship.

Coach Haskell had observed most of the Buffs' games and was amazed that they had won so many games especially during the tournament. He was also one of the naysayers who didn't give the Buffs the slightest chance to beat the Snow Canyon Warriors.

He was sharing his thoughts with the lady on his right from Morgan. She decided to stay after her team lost to Wasatch to see what Snow Canyon and Tooele looked like in order to evaluate, in her own mind, how Morgan might have matched up against them in a championship game. They were having a friendly discussion.

She was amazed that Haskell was so down on the Buffaloes but he was even more astounded when he learned the lady from Morgan believed the Buffs could beat Snow Canyon. She even volunteered to tell him she had attended the eighteen and forty-three point slaughters that Morgan inflicted on the Buffaloes during Region 11 games. They discussed the difference of opinions for a few moments but the lady couldn't point to any player from Tooele that encouraged her or any particular talent. She had an inkling that the Buffs could win. To explain her sentiment she finally related a story that impressed Coach Haskell:

"A few years ago our girls from Morgan High School were playing for the state championship. The game was close and very physical. Our coach always used the same five girls as starters and just one or two from the bench during the previous tournament games.

"Suddenly in the most important game of all he was sending in a girl that was well down the bench. The girl who came out of the game was a very valuable player on the team. The substitute girl continued to play throughout the third and fourth quarters while the starting player was still out of the game. I watched her off and on during the close game and every time I glanced in her direction she was cheering her heart out for the girl on the court. The girl was playing a great game but one of our best players remained on the bench to the end of a very tight game.

"The score was tied with less than thirty seconds left then we pulled ahead by three points. The other team shot a desperate but well aimed three-pointer that rattled back and forth inside the rim then it bounced against the backboard to roll around the rim a couple of times before it fell out with nine seconds left in the game. We held onto the ball to win the state championship.

"In celebration, the team eventually made it to the basket to cut down the net. The girls on the team took turns climbing a ladder to cut the strings until just one string was holding the net to the rim. The substitute girl's dad had the honor to climb the ladder to cut the last string. The net fell to the floor then it was picked up and put around the dad's neck. His family was hugging him and I noticed tears in everyone's eyes.

"In a few seconds I learned why the starter had sat out the championship game. It wasn't a brilliant decision made by the coach. Instead, the starter had requested that her best friend be given her playing time because her friend's dad would not live to see her play again. He had been diagnosed with a cancerous brain tumor!

"Both girls taught me a lesson that put basketball in perspective with the eternal significance of what life really means. Two weeks later I went to the man's funeral. They sang the song, "The Wind Beneath My Wings," with the words "Did you ever know that you were my hero?"

The lady's voice was weak and her eyes were glistening in the bright lights of the gymnasium. Large tears raced down her cheeks. She took a deep breath and wiped them away then continued, "I have watched hundreds of ballgames but this is the only one that I haven't forgotten. I don't know a lot about the intricacies of basketball or anything about the Tooele boys and the coaches, except that their head coach has a severe cancer. But I suspect they wouldn't have made it this far unless there is a purpose that is greater than either one of us can understand. They may play like angels with broken wings but I don't doubt destiny or what the Buffs can do!"

The story made an impression on Coach Haskell but he was embedded too deep in logic to be swayed from the ranks of the skeptics who stated publicly, "The Buffaloes are not even worthy of discussion as a contender in this tournament. They shouldn't even be here. This game will be a cake walk for the Warriors."

There was so little said about Tooele that many people were mispronouncing the name as Too-eel-lee. One by one the teams were introduced as they ran onto the court with high-fives and chest bumps. The band rose to the occasion with a musical crescendo for each player. When the Warriors were introduced the students from Tooele turned around with their backs to the crowd. A few purple shirts were seen that read, "Gary's Kids."

After the introductions, fifteen Buffs gathered in a circle at the center of the court with their hands resting on the shoulders of the players beside them. "FCA, FCA, FCA!" they shouted. Then they promised each other they would use every ounce of energy in the game - no matter how long they played or what the score was.

Coach Brown, of the Warriors was not caught up in the furor that took the Buffs for granted as losers. He was cautiously on the side of worry about what might happen in the game. Like the Tooele team at midcourt, his team was grouped in the same close circle in front of his bench but he was kneeling in the center. "Forget everything you have heard about Tooele. They are a very good team. They can put you under if you play less than your best, but I agree with you: they can be beat! Get the ball inside to Leavitt for a close shot or where he can work to draw a foul. Don't be taken out of our game. This is a very serious opponent."

It would be difficult but Coach Brown was determined to put his team in the proper frame of mind against the smaller and less powerful Buffaloes.

On the first play, the ball was tipped by Leavitt to Willard for a quick layup. Less than ten seconds into the game the Warriors were ahead of the Buffs 2-0. The lively Snow Canyon fans immediately went into a chant, "It's all over. It's all over. It's all over!" Just as fast, the Warriors had fallen victim to believing the chant and fifteen seconds into the game, Coach Brown would need to earn his big bucks. His players had blocked his warnings and advice out of their minds and were already listening to the experts. Both groups had already written off the Buffaloes as losers.

Coach Brown couldn't afford to rely on size, a great "money player," and an excellent team to beat the Buffs. He knew he needed every weapon in his arsenal to survive the spirit driven stampede of the Buffaloes. Arrogance and mental overconfidence would neutralize his superior weaponry. On defense, he yelled out to the court, "Stay on them, do not lighten up!" and on offense he yelled to deaf ears, "Work it inside, get it to Coby then drive in for a basket and a foul!" The Warriors could dominate the Buffs if they concentrated on using their senior, 6'10" Coby Leavitt, against the 6'5" sophomore from Tooele.

As if a signal was given, the coats and jackets were taken off by the Tooele students to expose hundreds of purple t-shirts that read, "The Herd" on the front and "Gary's Kids" on the back. Rumor was--the inspirational shirts were the idea of the high school secretaries but the origin remained as mysterious as the effect the shirts had on the players and fans of both teams. The shirts propelled the momentum in favor of the Buffs and temporarily backed the Warriors into a crouch allowing the tempo of the game to be dictated by Tooele.

Some relief was given to the Warriors when it became noticeable that the Morgan fans had stayed over after being beaten by Wasatch to cheer for them. If Morgan couldn't win the championship they would desperately support the next strong team that could stop Wasatch from winning. In this tournament the only team left that was good enough to do it was the Warriors. Of course, since Morgan was playing the next day for the consolation prize, it wouldn't hurt to have Tooele lose this game so they could use the Buffs for some more target practice. Maybe they could beat them by fifty points this time.

Tooele was unfazed by the shenanigans surrounding the court even though the Warriors were already on the scoreboard on the way to their fifty-nine points per game average. Both teams traded possession of the ball a few times without scoring and using several minutes off the clock. The Buffs finally broke the ice when Boucher launched a successful three-pointer. Lawrence made a steal then passed to Holt for another basket then Palmer made a free throw. Boucher made a basket and Tooele was where they wanted to be, leading 8-2 with a minute to play in the first quarter. The Warriors were showing signs of confusion but Frei made another basket before the quarter ended to bring them within four. The score was 8-4.

The scoring was higher in the second quarter but the pace was probably slower as the Buffs were more determined to control the ball and play a tough zone defense. The "money player" for the Warriors who had scored twenty-five points the night before didn't even take a shot in the first quarter. The Warriors worked hard to get the ball inside but Leavitt was either guarded or forced out of position to take it inside. Eventually he got the ball twice, but he appeared to rush his shot both times as if he was afraid he wouldn't get another opportunity to score. Another time he was fouled and made one of two free throws. In two quarters Leavitt had a grand total of one point.

The Buffs scored a three pointer by Lockie who back-peddled down the court pointing one finger toward the Tooele students and the band. They went wild but Frei silenced them with a basket and Mulford made a three pointer. With Leavitt's free throw the Warriors were within one. The score favored Tooele 11-10. The possessions went back and forth again;

both teams made many passes. The announcers were calling the game boring. This was supposed to be run-and-gun high school basketball.

Tooele made so many passes on one possession that the announcers declared the Buffs' game plan was to lull everybody to sleep then zap them with a surprise shot at the basket to wake them up. Lawrence woke them up with a basket for the Buffs then Lockie made two free throws before Frei made another basket for the Warriors. The score was 15-12. Coming down the stretch to end the half, the Buffs scored a basket by Palmer, two free throws by Lockie, and a free throw by the hard-working Alex Despain.

The Warriors' Frei made a desperate shot just a fraction of a second after the buzzer and it didn't count. Frei stayed on the court to plead his case to the refs but they said the shot was taken after the buzzer. It was a painful half for the Warriors. Now it was Tooele 20 and Snow Canyon 12.

Sometimes a player's greatest challenge is coming to grips with his role on the team.

Scottie Pippen

Champions aren't made in the gyms. Champions are made from something they have deep inside them--a desire, a dream, a vision.

]Muhammad Ali

When I step onto the court, I don't have to think about anything. If I have a problem off the court, I find that after I play, my mind is clearer and I can come up with a better solution. It's like therapy. It relaxes me and allows me to solve problems.

Michael Jordan

Chapter Nineteen
Three Teams Standing

It's the thrill of the fight rising up to the challenge of our rival
and the last known survivor stalks his prey in the night!
Eye of the Tiger--Survivor

The two coaches worked the court throughout the first half: Coach Alverson stood calmly in front of his chair and appeared to be pleased with the performance of his team. Coach Brown knelt down in front of his chair and appeared to plead to his players continuously to convince them to follow his game plan. To his dismay the high-scoring Warriors had scored an anemic twelve points in two quarters and his All-State player had just one point.

The teams are allowed fifteen players and five coaches to sit at courtside as a team. The Warriors had an interesting arrangement of coaches. The two sitting on the far right side next to the scorer's table had a suspicious interest in the lone Tooele cheerleader with the two pigtails. She was cheering and waving her pom-poms on the court with the eyes of the two coaches glued to her. The coaches were dressed in ties and perfectly pressed white shirts with clipboards in their hands. On closer inspection the two coaches had crew-cuts just exactly like Coach Brown and they were both about ten-years-old. No one knew whether their father brought them courtside to help him with the game or if he brought his young sons to see Tooele's cheerleader. It was also apparent that the boys were well mannered and qualified to help their dad.

In the third quarter, Leavitt doubled his scoring pace by scoring one more point in just one quarter instead of two. The Warriors were back on track after a motivational uplift by Coach Brown. Tooele had increased the lead to nine points on a basket by Lockie, 22-13, but the Warriors exploded for eight points in less than two minutes. A three-pointer by Hurst and Willard and free throws by Willard and Frei brought them back within one point of Tooele, 22-21. Halfway through the third quarter the Warriors were neck-and-neck with the floundering Buffs.

More than two and one-half quarters filled with miscues, hurried shots, and closed ears to Coach Brown's instructions had been forgiven. At any moment the power-packed Warriors could streak ahead with their high powered offense. The ball went to Tooele's Castle for his second attempt of the night, a three-pointer that pumped up the Buffs' adrenalin when it was needed the most. The score was Tooele 25 and Snow Canyon 21.

Leavitt increased his scoring total by fifty percent when he made another free throw, he had three points. A minute later he made a surprising put back to end the third quarter with five points. Lockie made a basket and a free throw. Then a Warrior hit another two point basket after the buzzer. It was ruled to be late and did not count. When the third quarter ended the Warriors had finally outscored the Buffs in a quarter to cut Tooele's lead, 28-24.

The Warriors were well within striking distance on the slightest mistake by a Buffalo but four points seemed like ten to Snow Canyon. They were barely forty percent of their average and three quarters were gone. The Buffs had paralyzed them and they didn't like it. They were beginning to worry, to dwell on the officiating, and they were overreacting to the frustrations created by the well-disciplined Tooele team. Coach Brown recognized the pit his team was digging for themselves so he put his soul into his most inspirational speech to motivate his team. The players eyes darted back and forth at each other, they bounced up and down in nervousness, and they turned in different directions for no apparent reason, but they acted like they understood his plea.

On Tooele's side of the court the players were standing alert and attentive in a circle around their coach. Coach was where he wanted to be and he had a four point lead.

The final quarter started with a quick basket by Lawrence then the Warriors added four points on a surprising surge by Leavitt increasing his total to nine points counting his one point in the first half. The score stood at Tooele 30 and Snow Canyon 28. Lawrence made another two then the Warriors' Frei had the ball with the opportunity to trim the lead to two points. Under intense defensive pressure from Holt, he overreacted in frustration to intentionally shove Holt out of bounds. The ref called a flagrant offensive foul and Holt made both free throws. Instead of a two point game the flagrant foul resulted in a four point swing for Tooele to increase their lead, 34-28. This was a crucial turning point in the game.

The Warriors' Anderson made a three and Willard made a free throw, 34-32. Lockie made two free throws for Tooele. Frei made two free throws for the Warriors. Lockie made two more free throws then Frei made a two point basket. Boucher made two free throws during a quick in and out of the game appearance for the Buffs. Castle made two free throws for Tooele. A basket by Willard and a basket by Frei brought the Warriors within two, 42-40 with less than a minute to play.

The Buffs were in ball control mode, as usual, and an impatient decision or a miscue would be deadly. The Warriors had applied intense defensive pressure at unpredictable times that was very effective at causing the Buffs to lose the ball but the Warriors were the impatient ones. During the previous quarter they had argued and routed more of their concentration toward the referees than to the Buffaloes. The more they disputed the calls the more anxious the referees were to blow the whistle against them. The Buffs had been saved from turnovers on at least two occasions by controversial fouls. On another occasion the refs missed an obvious over and back by Holt at the half court line. The unrestrained Warriors fouled again: this time Holt hit one of two foul shots, 43-40.

The Warriors had possession of the ball with thirty-five seconds remaining. Coach Brown called time out then forgot all about his team to argue old calls with the referees. He gave his most animated plea to the referees but his efforts fell on deaf ears. Meanwhile, a livid assistant coach took over, waving his arms as he explained the situation to the Warriors, "Work the ball quickly to the inside. Let Coby use his height to score two or maybe draw a foul for three. Don't rush yet, but if you have an open three, take it. On defense, do not allow them to waste our time. If you can't steal a transition or inbounds pass then foul asap. Do not foul Holt or Lockie, or Boucher if he is in the game unless it is necessary. The Buffs are a poor foul shooting team so if we foul the worst of them we can still have two or three chances to make up a measly three points."

During the time out on the Tooele side, Coach put his best free throw shooters in the game. He did this in the final minutes of every game when the Buffs had the lead. All five coaches were chewing gum so rapidly there wasn't much opportunity for words to slip out. Finally, Coach instructed the Buffs; "Do not foul, defend your areas. No matter what the Warriors do on this possession we will either be ahead or tied with very few seconds remaining - maybe fifteen seconds - so let the air out of the ball and make your foul shots. We can win one!"

The Warriors rushed a poor three-point shot so quickly that Leavitt must have been invisible to them. They immediately fouled Castle who hit two free throws. The Warriors turned over the ball then immediately fouled Castle again who hit another two free throws. The desperate Warriors threw up another long three-point shot and Palmer out-jumped Leavitt for the rebound. With eight ticks on the clock the Warriors could see their life flash before their eyes. One of them grabbed Palmer. He made two more free throws to end the scoring; Tooele 49 and Snow Canyon 40.

The Tooele High School Band sent out a hymn of jubilation that filled the E-Center. The Sha-Ronns, the White Buffalo, Kyle McKendrick, Danny Wihongi, Blake Olsen, and the little cheerleader were smothered on the court by the Tooele students and fans. Everyone who had been rooting for the Warriors stood or sat motionless like statues of salt. Most of them had both hands on their head and were looking toward the rafters with their eyes closed in disbelief.

Coby Leavitt had scored seventy-nine points in the three other games in the tournament but Tooele had held him to nine. Twenty players scored more points during the tournament than Nash Lockie, the game's highest scorer for Tooele.

Everyone loves a winner but no winner is loved more than one who comes from behind; the one who is not given a chance to win, but overcomes demoralizing odds to find a way to win anyway.

This championship game would resemble the fights in the coliseums during Biblical times. The weakened saints would face the strong and starving lions. It wouldn't be much of a fight. The David of the tournament with odds of twenty to one against them would face the Goliath of the tournament. Wasatch had won the state championship two years in a row. Most fans believed the win against Morgan made them the state champions three years in a row.

During an interview after the game Coach Brown talked about more than just basketball. He had won big games that led to championships and he had felt the disappointments of defeat. "We were the heavy favorite with everything to lose but Tooele had nothing to lose. They had already achieved much more than they were expected. I was worried about playing them because they were playing for something else: a coach with cancer. I believe they played for a higher cause and their coach was the instrument to teach greater principles than those that stay on a basketball court to be isolated in the world of basketball.

"In this tournament everything aligned just right, the benefits from winning the coin toss to determine their position in the brackets could not be greater. Everything went their way after the flip of the coin, in every game. There were controversial calls, their opponents had perfect shots that rolled back out, their shots fell like heart stopping daggers at the most important times for them, they were fouled at the same time they were committing turnovers, the buzzers took away opponents baskets, and they would beat the buzzers. When the team gathered at midcourt before the game and shouted, "FCA", my heart sank because I immediately knew what it stood for. The Buffs were filled with innocence and worthy of big things. I am not sure they even understood the full meaning of their destiny.

"Tooele is a "Team of Destiny." No team that has played them in the last five or six games can deny it. I believe all those things: divine intervention happens, an angel is watching over them, and I look forward to see what fate awaits them tomorrow afternoon. Wasatch is an exceptionally strong team. In the state there are ten to twelve teams much better than Tooele and none of them can beat Wasatch right now."

2001-2002 was Coach Brown's first year at Snow Canyon. His young freshman coach named Mark had died of a heart attack, and his son, Jordan, was a guard on the varsity team in 2005. The whole team dedicated that season to Mark and they wore a black shoulder band as a reminder. They had lost to Dixie during the season twice, once by 23 points. But they played Dixie again in the semi final game and beat them by twenty. He said, "I know that Mark was watching over us and he was guiding our team's shots through the basket."

The Snow Canyon Warriors weren't very tough in 2002 but took third in region and had to play Emery in Castledale to make it to the state tournament. The Warriors won by sixteen. For the first game in the tournament they should have played Morgan (22-0) but for some strange reason Union beat Morgan at Morgan in double overtime 88-84, so Snow Canyon ended up playing Union. They beat Union, 61-39. In the semi-final game they beat Dixie 57-37. At last, they played for the championship against Pine View. Snow Canyon had beat them the first time they met during the season, 69-61, and then got stomped the second time they played, 77-63. Coach Brown continued, "I know Mark was up there helping us out again and our players felt that way too. It took all of us to beat Pine View in the State Championship, 59-54."

Snow Canyon was coached by a very honorable man who set rules of conduct that he expected to be followed by his team. Coach Brown was convinced that the character of his players was more important than winning any game. His Warriors beat the Buffs earlier in the year largely because they had a terrific player named Nigel Moore. But Nigel violated a rule and could not play in the semi-final game against Tooele. He was allowed to accompany the team on the bench and he put his whole heart into the game as he cheered his teammates on.

Coach Brown and the Warriors had overlooked Tooele by setting their sights on either Morgan or Wasatch in the championship game. He and his team were overconfident. Nigel was definitely out but they believed they could win without him anyway, because the Buffs were not a good team. He even told his players the coach of the Tooele team had cancer, which he later regretted. Just before the tipoff he realized his mistakes but it was too late to refocus his team for the game. He kept trying throughout the entire game but it couldn't be done.

There were a few encouraging cheers but jeers against the Buffs were more common when they went outside the E Center after the game. A bold voice boomed through the freezing air. "Hey Mike Holt, your brother Matt caught a pass to beat us in the football championship game in 2002. That ain't gonna happen again. We will beat you worse than your embarrassing loss to Morgan by forty-three points. You and your buddies can't find enough heroes in all of Tooele to keep us from winning our third basketball championship in a row tomorrow night!"

The newspapers reported very little about the Tooele-Snow Canyon game but they couldn't print enough about the Wasatch-Morgan game with its "money players." It was declared the 3A State Championship Game as far as they were concerned. Wasatch was even crowned by the media as the new state champion on Friday night.

Any of the five players on the starting team for Wasatch would be the "money player" if they were on Tooele's team. The Buffs had a team of five starters but it was the twenty-fifth game of the year and they were still changing the starting lineup. Both teams would go through the motions but it was time for the real game to begin: there would be no mercy extended to Tooele, who many thought shouldn't be in the tournament anyway. Everyone knew Wasatch was going to kill Tooele on Saturday afternoon, in the most embarrassing game ever played for a 3A State Championship.

The players and fans from Morgan had a tendency to be haughty towards Tooele. They had certainly stomped the Buffs twice and their 24-1 record was certainly more impressive than Tooele's 16-8, but they had blown the opportunity to win the state championship. Many of them were taking out their frustrations with flippant remarks aimed at the Buffs instead of the team that had beaten them. It seemed like they were blaming the Buffs for their failure. It was easier to dislike the Buffs for playing in the championship game than admit Wasatch had beaten them. Morgan had wanted to play Tooele really bad.

The newspapers reported four or five players from three of the top four teams would be moving on to continue playing basketball at the college level. Then they added the fourth team was Tooele and none of the Buffs were moving on.

Leadership is the art of getting someone else to do something you want done because he wants to do it.
Dwight Eisenhower

Setting an example is not the main means of influencing others; it is the only means.
Albert Einstein

Chapter Twenty
Two Coaches' Chessboard of Gladiators

It's all on the line, this is the place, and this is the time.
You waited forever, it's now or it's never. Nothing can stop you
now.
Moment Of Truth--Survivor

The boys walked into the E Center with a win on their mind. They were thankful their biggest fear had been eliminated by their new enemy, the Wasatch Wasps. Morgan was gone and the Buffs were one of two teams that remained in the race for the 3A State Championship. They had dreaded playing Morgan again after two embarrassing losses to them during the season. And they had spent a lot of time worrying how they could get past them in the tournament.

They had not given up and the rest was taken care of, just like Coach had told them it would be. In this case Coach had taken care of the problematic Morgan team with one simple coin toss. The Buffs' could never be grateful enough that a coin had put them in a different tournament bracket than Morgan, at least until the brackets merged together in the championship game. The two-time reigning champions from Wasatch bumped Morgan out of the running by six points.

Who would have believed the Buffs would be dressed in their basketball jerseys ready to play ball in the E Center on the last day of the state tournament? More than that, they had won some impressive games against Ben Lomond, Bear River, Granite, Dixie, and Snow Canyon, but who would have thought they would be ready to play the two-time defending champions who were strong enough to beat Morgan?

Tooele was a tough bunch to understand but that is something they had endured since the season started. There had been one unexpected event after another but they always moved forward.

The Wasatch team repeated the statement that they had won the state championship by beating Morgan the night before. Coach mentioned it when he talked to his team before the game, "The Wasps are a great team but don't let that stop you. We want to be the champions that beat the best opponent in the state. We want to play the Wasps."

Coach wrote something on his whiteboard with his blue marker. The team was surprised when he turned it to face them. It read, "Wasatch said they won the championship yesterday by beating Morgan!"

Coach continued, "We can't allow that statement to pass us by. What do you say? Can the Wasps beat us that easily?"

He wrote again on his whiteboard knowing what the boys expected. Before turning the board toward them he asked "What did I write?"

The Buffs had won five in a row so one of them answered, "5-0."

Coach turned the board around again to reveal, "0-0."

The boys looked surprised so he explained to them, "All of those games are behind us. We are moving forward with one game of importance: the championship game. We are thirty point underdogs. If we win, you will always be 1-0. If we lose, all of us go back where we started at 0-0 to start moving forward from the beginning again."

It was a shattering blow to think about enduring everything they had experienced during the season for nothing but a 0-0 record. One of the many team leaders named Nash Lockie responded to Coach's challenge, "We aren't happy just to be here."

Then the rest of the players joined him, "We want it all. We can win one!"

The Buffs were ready to rumble.

Citizens from Tooele flooded into the E-Center with as many as the number of fans from Wasatch. Several thousand spectators had a feeling deep inside that the game might not be a slaughter.

None of the spectators arrived before Ms. Syra and the THS Band. Every member of the band was wearing a purple shirt that read on the front "The Herd" and on the back "Gary's Kids." They were already seated in chairs on the court behind a basket. They intended to greet the fans with some extra pep to increase the excitement level even more.

A new fan in a purple shirt was in the stands to see his very first basketball game. In fact, he claimed it was the first ballgame, of any kind he had ever attended in his entire life. Darren, from Coach's history class, was sitting one row behind Coach and they were talking about something important. It was later learned that Coach had reserved that exact seat for Darren. Coach was wearing his black shirt and tie, he had his arms swinging, and he was pointing at different things on the court. At the same time the expressions on Darren's face kept changing from bewildered to a look that appeared to mean he understood what Coach was telling him.

Suddenly, Darren pulled out his cell phone and it looked like he was either threatening to use it or he did use it. If he punched a text message on it then he must have done it very quickly. This made Coach look like he was bewildered until he suddenly changed his expression to look like he understood what Darren was telling him. They both laughed, Coach turned to concentrate on his team, and Darren definitely began text messaging on his cell phone.

One of the cheerleaders from the Wasps ran down the side of the court carrying a poster that read, "Sting the Buffs."

The ever-energetic White Buffalo was on the court wearing a purple shirt, waving and shouting cheers back and forth with the crowd.

Next to the White Buffalo, the smallest of all purple shirts was worn by a little cheerleader with two dark pigtails waving a pom-pom with each hand.

Within a few minutes, more than half the crowd was seated on one side of the court wearing the same type of purple shirts. "The Herd" was printed on the front of the shirt and "Gary's Kids" was printed on the back. Purple shirts continued to enter the building. The entire side of the court looked like it was covered with a purple blanket but right in the middle was a small white spot that caught everyone's eye; Coach Haskell's wife, Tina, was wearing a white shirt. Later, when questioned about the white shirt, she explained, "The memo to wear a purple "The Herd" shirt was the only memo I have ever missed in my entire life!"

The Tooele cheerleaders were basking in the sunshine in Ft. Lauderdale, Florida, but the three number one fans were on the court wearing purple shirts. Danny was holding a poster: "Wasp's can't sting, they fly for cover!"

The Buffs completed the layup drill and were lining up around the three-point line to shoot some long warm up shots as the clock slowly ticked down to tipoff time.

One by one the players were introduced from each team. The bands from each school alternated a musical crescendo in conjunction with their player running onto the court for high fives and chest bumps with their teammates.

When the Tooele team was introduced, the fans from Wasatch turned their backs to the court to imitate what the Buffs' fans had done the night before at the Snow Canyon game. The Buffs' fans were not to be out done so easily. When the Wasps were introduced the Buffs' fans pulled out newspapers and opened them up wide so their entire section looked like one big newspaper.

A slight disturbance occurred in the bleachers in the Tooele section. Three boys from another high school had succeeded in getting exact replicas of the purple shirts made but theirs had "The Herd" written on the front inside a big circle with a line slashing through the lettering. The security officers rounded them up and escorted them out of sight. The shirts were never seen again.

After the introductions the Tooele team circled at midcourt again. This time they pumped their hands then shouted clearly into the air, "For Coach Alverson!" Then they ran to their bench.

The game started off in typical Tooele fashion: the Wasps missed several attempts and the Buffs played patiently with twenty to thirty passes per possession but they didn't score. Three minutes into the game Mike Holt scored a free throw, Josh Boucher made a steal, then Nash Lockie drove in to score. The Wasps tried to get the ball inside to their two big men but were forced to settle for longer shots that failed. Holt hit a jumper from fifteen feet to put the Buffs ahead, 5-0.

During preliminary discussions before the game the announcers mentioned the surprise that the Buffs made it past game one in the playoffs. Now, they were leading the power packed Wasatch Wasps halfway through the first quarter.

Tooele committed three turnovers and missed some shots in what remained of the quarter. Meanwhile the Wasps went on a tear, scoring ten unanswered points that put the Buffs back in the world of the underdog. Before the quarter ended Holt made another free throw. The score was 10-6.

The Wasps planned to put the Buffs away in the second quarter but five different players (Lockie, Alex Despain, Josh Boucher, Holt, and Colton Hogan) scored baskets for the Buffs including a timely three point bomb by Holt. For the Wasps, Mahoney scored four more points and Magnusson scored two. In his first appearance in the playoffs, Despain out fought the giants of Wasatch for three offensive and three defensive rebounds to beat the Wasps at their own game. The Buffs took the lead with the score at the half, 19-18.

The announcers were shell-shocked, "Tooele is a team that many thought should not be here today and Wasatch is a superior team that beat the best last night. Tonight is supposed to be a thirty point blowout but the Buffs have postponed the sting of the Wasps until the second half. The Buffs keep bending but they come right back so they must be feeling good about themselves. They have the lead."

One of the 3A State Basketball Academic Awards was presented to Alex Despain at halftime. Despain had made a big contribution to his team in the game but his excellence in his studies was an achievement that only a handful of players had earned. Earlier in the year, Cody Castle and Alex Despain were recipients of the Region Basketball Academic Award.

In the second half the Wasps charged back into the lead as Mahoney and Woodruff made six quick points. Taylor Palmer made a free throw for the Buffs then Mahoney made two more. At midpoint of the third quarter the score favored Wasatch, 26-20.

The Wasps were headed toward the celebration at the hive. The Buffs' fans were silent. It was time to put the Buffs away; the Wasp cheerleaders were leading the crowd to further intimidate the Tooele boys on the court. The cheerleaders would shout, "Buzzzz." Then the fans from Wasatch would echo loudly, "Buzzzz."

Not to be outdone, Danny Wihongi was always prepared. He pulled out a poster to wave back at the Wasatch crowd, "Buzzzz" in Wasp means, "Look Out!"

A six point lead was a mountain to climb with th... offense, but if the Wasps forced them out of their game compound their problem. The Wasps were too big and t... up with in a fast-paced game. But suddenly Holt score... an alert Taylor Palmer made a steal, then Larkin scored desperate long shot by the Wasps was h... by Palmer to Holt for another two points. The Buffs were suddenly... benefactors of a fast-paced game. In less than two minutes... stormed back to tie the game, 26-26

With the game tied Tooele went back to a slow tempo... out rebounded the Buffs seven to one in the quarter. Tooele... an offensive rebound in the quarter and just one defensive... while Malinkey recovered him. When the Buffs missed a shot... on automatic change of possession to the Wasps. Tyler Baird hit a point at the buzzer to break the tie in favor of Wasatch 29-16.

"Tooele bends but Wasatch can't break them. Three quarters... been played in the championship game and Tooele, like a bad dream th... won't go away is still hanging on," reported the sports announcer.

In the fourth quarter, Magnusson hit two free throws and the score was 31-26. The tempo of the game remained slow. Every pass, every shot, and every whistle was critical for both teams. The Wasps still lead at 35-31 with 5:03 to play. They had another opportunity to put the Buffs away but Palmer took the ball straight at the Wasps' big man for a layup. The Wasps made a free throw. A play later Palmer hit another timely shot over the outstretched arms of two big men from Wasatch. They were important shots to boost the sinking Buffs, and Holt hit for two points to tie the Wasps. The score was 35-35 with four minutes to play.

Coach motioned for Colton Hogan from the bench. He jumped up and immediately ran to Coach while he was in the process of removing a warm-up jersey. Coach was focused with every mental fiber on the game. He reached for Hogan to push him toward the court for substitution, just like he had done dozens of times with his players during the season. In a hurry to get into the game, he pulled off both his warm up shirt and his playing jersey. Before he realized his situation; he had thrown both shirts behind him and he stood bare-chested ten feet out on the court.

The crowd laughed and applauded him as he rushed back to the bench to put on his jersey. His pearl white skin had changed to crimson red.

Toole committed three turnovers and missed some shots in what remained of the quarter. Meanwhile the Wasps went on a tear, scoring ten unanswered points that put the Buffs back in the world of the underdog. Before the quarter ended Holt made another free throw. The score was 10-6.

The Wasps planned to put the Buffs away in the second quarter but five different players (Lockie, Alex Despain, Josh Boucher, Holt, and Colton Hogan) scored baskets for the Buffs including a timely three point bomb by Holt. For the Wasps, Mahoney scored four more points and Magnusson scored two. In his first appearance in the playoffs, Despain out fought the giants of Wasatch for three offensive and three defensive rebounds to beat the Wasps at their own game. The Buffs took the lead with the score at the half, 19-18.

The announcers were shell-shocked, "Tooele is a team that many thought should not be here today and Wasatch is a superior team that beat the best last night. Tonight is supposed to be a thirty point blowout but the Buffs have postponed the sting of the Wasps until the second half. The Buffs keep bending but they come right back so they must be feeling good about themselves. They have the lead."

One of the 3A State Basketball Academic Awards was presented to Alex Despain at halftime. Despain had made a big contribution to his team in the game but his excellence in his studies was an achievement that only a handful of players had earned. Earlier in the year, Cody Castle and Alex Despain were recipients of the Region Basketball Academic Award.

In the second half the Wasps charged back into the lead as Mahoney and Woodruff made six quick points. Taylor Palmer made a free throw for the Buffs then Mahoney made two more. At midpoint of the third quarter the score favored Wasatch, 26-20.

The Wasps were headed toward the celebration at the hive. The Buffs' fans were silent. It was time to put the Buffs away; the Wasp cheerleaders were leading the crowd to further intimidate the Tooele boys on the court. The cheerleaders would shout, "Buzzzz." Then the fans from Wasatch would echo loudly, "Buzzzz."

Not to be outdone, Danny Wihongi was always prepared. He pulled out a poster to wave back at the Wasatch crowd, "Buzzz," in Wasp means, "Look Out!"

A six point lead was a mountain to climb with the slow-paced Toole offense, but if the Wasps forced them out of their game plan, they could compound their problem. The Wasps were too big and too good to keep up with in a fast-paced game. But suddenly Holt scored a two pointer, an alert Taylor Palmer made a steal, then Lockie scored two more. A desperate long shot by the Wasps was rebounded by Palmer then passed to Holt for another two points. The Buffs were suddenly the surprised benefactors of a faster paced game. In less than two minutes they had stormed back to tie the game, 26-26.

With the game tied Toole went back to a slow offense. Wasatch out rebounded the Buffs seven to one in the quarter. Toole never got an offensive rebound in the quarter and just one defensive rebound while Mahoney recovered four. When the Buffs missed a shot it was an automatic change of possession to the Wasps. Tyler Baird hit a three pointer at the buzzer to break the tie in favor of Wasatch 29-26.

"Toole bends but Wasatch can't break them. Three quarters have been played in the championship game and Toole, like a bad dream that won't go away, is still hanging on," reported the sports announcer.

In the fourth quarter, Magnusson made two free throws and the score was 31-26. The tempo of the game remained slow. Every pass, every shot, and every whistle was critical for both teams. The Wasps still lead at 35-31 with 5:22 to play. They had another opportunity to put the Buffs away but Palmer took the ball straight at the Wasps' big man for a layup. The Wasps made a free throw. A play later Palmer hit another timely shot over the outstretched arms of two big men from Wasatch. They were important shots to boost the sinking Buffs, and Holt hit for two points to tie the Wasps. The score was 35-35 with four minutes to play.

Coach motioned for Colton Hogan from the bench. He jumped up and immediately ran to Coach while he was in the process of removing a warm-up jersey. Coach was focused with every mental fiber on the game. He reached for Hogan to push him toward the court for substitution, just like he had done dozens of times with his players during the season. In a hurry to get into the game, he pulled off both his warm up shirt and his playing jersey. Before he realized his situation; he had thrown both shirts behind him and he stood bare-chested ten feet out on the court.

The crowd laughed and applauded him as he rushed back to the bench to put on his jersey. His pearl white skin had changed to crimson red.

The Wasps held the ball, content to take a page from the Buffs' playbook: they wanted the last shot, a perfect opportunity to score, or some foul shots. With a little more than a minute remaining in the game the Buffs were guilty of committing a foul. Mahoney made one of two foul shots. The score was 36-35 then Tooele lost the ball. The Wasps were back in the driver's seat, the clock was on their side and to the dismay of the Buffaloes, it was ticking rapidly toward the final buzzer. The Buffs played defense for fifteen seconds but could not steal the ball from the patient Wasps. Wasatch was content to hold the ball. They finally had the game wrapped up and it was too late for the pesky Buffs to do anything about it.

With twenty-five seconds on the clock Castle intentionally fouled a Wasp. Tooele called a time-out, hoping to add pressure on an excellent free throw shooter from Wasatch. The Wasps had the game with a chance to further increase their lead.

"It's over," shouted the announcer, "It's over and what a great run it has been for Tooele. The odds against them were staggering and they carried an unbearable weight on their young shoulders all year long. They bent but they didn't break but in the end; the media and naysayers were right when they said the Buffs couldn't do it. We have a great Cinderella story anyway. Even though the Wasatch Wasps have put the clamps on a victory for the championship, the second place Buffs have had an amazing run that outdistanced their wildest dreams."

Another sports announcer added, "That is exactly correct. Wasatch was an unbeatable foe for a weaker but well disciplined Tooele team. Many say they shouldn't even have been in the tournament. It was an uphill battle for the Buffs. In fact, it was a miracle for them to even make it to this championship game. Their parents, school, community and coach should be very proud of their accomplishment. Being runner-up to the Wasps is nothing to shake a stick at! The Wasps are a powerhouse. That is why they have three-peated their reign as champions for the third year in a row."

"The teams are back on the court," the first announcer responded as he took back the microphone. "I guess we agree totally. I recognize the incredible talent the Wasps have to dominate the 3A League, but I must admit that I appreciate the great showing of support the Tooele fans have exhibited tonight for a great group of boys. The joy I feel for the Wasps in winning, is equal to the pain and respect that I feel for the Buffs in losing."

In this game, a one point lead and shooting foul shots with a little more than twenty seconds remaining was a deep pit to be in. Against the tall and talented Wasps, the Buffs weren't just in a hole but a back-hoe was backfilling the dirt.

"He is on the line ready to shoot. There it goes. It's a brick! It's a brick!" repeated the announcer, overwhelmed with the excitement. "The ball hit the base on top of the basket against the glass and dropped into the waiting hands of Hogan. He throws an outlet pass to Lockie. He hits Holt charging desperately down the court. Instead of being down by two or three points the Buffs are only down by one, but time is running out. Four Wasps collapse on him, to prevent any possibility of a basket, with another Wasp on his heels. There is nowhere for Holt to go and no Buffs are under the basket for him to pass to. The Wasps have won it! They have won the game! They have stopped the Buffs again! Holt is surrounded at the top of the key in the Wasps' control. The clock is ticking. The Wasps have their third championship in as many years, a prized three-peat. There is not enough time for the Buffs to be patient now. A teammate needs to get open under the basket. Holt needs some help. The tall timber from the Wasatch forest is all he can see.

"Out of the corner of his eye, Holt catches a glimpse of a dark jersey on a teammate waving his hands above his head like he is unaware how little time is on the clock. No one is with him, he wants the ball. Holt passes the ball in desperation. I should have known: It's Cody Castle at his favorite spot on the court. He caught the pass from Holt and as he turns to face the basket, he shoots. He didn't aim; he just threw the ball up for grabs toward the basket. It's trailing toward the basket as if it is suspended in time. It looks way off; Magnusson, Woodruff, and Mahoney are waiting below the basket for the rebound and the 3A State Championship Title.

"The crowd is on their feet in front of our booth, the ball is flying in a high arch. It is curving slightly and diving toward the basket. It's difficult to see. I see it. The ball didn't hit anything, just the inside of the net, a bull's eye. The Buffs won it! Cody Castle hit the biggest shot in the history of Utah High School Basketball. He did it! Castle just threw the biggest dagger in Buffalo history. A miracle shot straight to the heart of the Wasps. Castle is already jumping up and down at half court. He looks like his feet have just been released from chains in cement on the bottom of the ocean."

"The four jubilant Buffaloes on the court are surrounding him, all of them jumping for joy. The underdogs have won and no one will be able to explain why," shouted the second announcer. "Hold on. Hold onto your seats. This game is not over yet. Coach Magnusson has just called a time-out with 12.5 seconds left to play."

Suddenly the E Center went deadly quiet. Coach Magnusson was a fearless master of the game with five fantastic players. If anyone was capable of scoring within twelve seconds, it was the Wasps. Tooele had scored three points in less time and Wasatch just needed two points to tie. Everyone knew he was prepared with a play designed for his big man under the basket.

"The teams are lining up in front of the Wasp' bench," the announcer began. "They make their moves. The play doesn't go inside. The Wasp coach has outsmarted everyone; the ball is inbounded to Burns, his scrappy guard, at half court. He is the smallest but fastest player on the court.

His big guys are setting up a wall of double and even triple screens. Burns has lost Castle, his assigned defender, and has a free lane to the basket. As fast as Castle became a hero, Burns is taking it from him to become the next legend for Wasatch. Burns drives in then jumps toward the glass for an uncontested layup. He missed it! The ball hits about every location inside the rim before bouncing out. Woodruff catches the ball for an easy put back. It hits the front and the back of the rim then it bounces out. He misses it. The Buffs win!

Wait! The ball is on the floor. There is a scramble for the ball. Holt falls on it. The game is over! Whistles and screams are everywhere. Wait a minute. I don't know who won or who is winning. Holt was touching the out of bounds line when he dove on the ball. The Wasps are barely alive with the ball out of bounds and 1.3 seconds remaining."

This time, Coach Magnusson the master magician, had to put all of his chips on the table. He had two and maybe three or more of the best players in 3A basketball, two straight state championships on the line, and a memory that no longer celebrated a win against Morgan. He had to go to his "money player."

There was a feeling of great respect and pride for the Buffaloes; they had fought bravely during an entire season right up to the wire with 1.3 seconds remaining. It was a great accomplishment to roam where the herd had never been before but anticipation and momentum favored the talented Wasps again.

The Buffs followed Coach's instructions to force the Wasp "money player" as far from the basket as possible when it was inbounded just in front of the Wasp's basket. Nonetheless, they were very aware that Coach Magnusson had just fooled them very badly. His designated play had resulted in two excellent opportunities right under the basket, surprisingly his team missed both shots. A pair of miracles had saved the Buffaloes for a few more seconds. The Wasps would never give up. The clock that had moved so quickly against the Buffs now was in the Wasps favor with a lifetime remaining, 1.3 seconds.

The players on both teams were very physical as they fought for position before the referees settled the disputes and handed the ball to be inbounded by a Wasp who was in back of the line.

The announcers sprang into action when the Wasp, standing out of bounds, slapped the basketball to begin a play designed by his coach. "It's a high and perfect lob pass, over the Buffs, aimed for Mahoney the tallest player on the court. Everyone jumps but Mahoney is an arm's length higher than them all. His outstretched hands catch the ball. Mahoney jumps right back up to shoot a fade away jump shot from eight feet out.

"It falls short. He missed it! Oh no, it was a perfect play at the perfect time to make history. It was working perfectly and no one anticipated it to fall short," shouts the announcer. "He should have driven it home for a layup, to draw foul shots, or even better, a layup and a foul shot. The ball fell short of the basket. He missed it! The Buffs win! Wasatch missed another golden opportunity to score. There are no whistles; lost in the noise is the sound of the final buzzer. The eruption you hear is being felt all over the state. The E Center feels like an earthquake from the Wasatch Fault is hitting 9.0 on the Richter scale!

"Tooele has beaten everyone, on and off the court. The new 3A State Champions will send shockwaves and aftershocks throughout the world of basketball for years to come!" Then the announcer was drowned out by the noise for a few moments.

This is the biggest high school game since the surprising Milan Indians, the real Hoosiers, pulled out a miracle to win the Indiana State Championship game in 1954, which became one of the greatest inspirational movies of all time named "Hoosiers." That was fifty-one years ago. Bobby Plump made a "shot heard 'round the world" for Milan then and Cody Castle made a "shot heard 'round the world" today in modern times. None of the Tooele boys and very few of their parents were born in 1954. Their coach was eight years old and running wild back then.

The announcer could be heard again, "The Buffs have won the championship. Coach Alverson is jumping up and down like he was still in high school. He's hugging his assistant coaches and everyone in reach. He is pointing at his kids on the team, his kids in the band, and his kids in the student section. This is a sports story ladies and gentlemen and all sports fans. He is a true champion!"

The final horn signaled an explosive celebration like no other ever experienced in THS history. Astonishment rippled through the capacity crowd at the E Center cheering for Tooele. There were tears and cheers and everything in between coming from the crowd. Some of the spectators who had rooted for the Wasps were suddenly clapping for the Buffs. Coach and his assistant coaches all hugged together in front of the bench while they were still jumping up and down. The court was filled with jubilant fans who were celebrating their first state championship in basketball.

In the center of the court the pile of the Tooele team who was hugging in celebration as they finally understood the reality of their accomplishment. All of them had been freed from the weight on their shoulders that they carried all season long. This was the end of the trail, there were no more games. They were the reigning 3A State Champions.

The only students remaining in their seats were the band and only half of them had fought the impulse to charge onto the court. Ms. Syra was still leading those that remained in a musical march that fueled greater excitement. The band had been a powerful support to the team of underdogs. The first to recognize them for that support was Coach. No one could stop him from hurrying to Ms. Syra to thank her with a hug and to give two thumbs up to the band before the herd pushed him forward to cut down the net. Each boy climbed the ladder to cut a string off the net for a souvenir then, Coach climbed up to cut the final string. He held it up to wave it above his head for the crowd to see and pointed to his players surrounding the ladder, "The players won it!"

Every conceivable emotion was displayed by the fans and every one of them was respectfully directed toward the Buffs in kindness. No one was sad or bitter. Some of the fans from the other schools were probably cheering secretly for the Buffs.

Coach Magnusson responded about the game, "That is why we play the game. Regardless of what the experts say, you can't predict the outcome. Tonight the Buffs were the spoiler and last night we were the spoiler against Morgan. 3A has some very good teams. I may have overlooked Tooele just like some other excellent teams did, but they deserve to win because of the way they played throughout the tournament and especially in this championship game. I have lost some big games before and some close games that made me feel bad. The game tonight couldn't have been any bigger for Wasatch and it couldn't have been any closer. This loss is tough like all losses are, but I don't feel as bad for losing to the Buffaloes from Tooele who against all odds have never given up. They have played for a higher cause. My players played with all they had right up to the very end but we came up a basket short. Everything lined up perfectly for the Buffs and they couldn't be beat. I have played some determined teams before, but after seeing with my own eyes what transpired tonight. I am a believer. Tooele was a "Team of Destiny!" Congratulations and good luck to them and Coach Alverson."

It was obvious what road led to the championship this year. 3A basketball was loaded with an exceptional caliber of "money players" but this time the road of destiny was the right one. The entire crowd at the E Center had been converted. The Buffs truly were a "Team of Destiny."

Shouts echoed through the E Center, "We won one!" and chants of "Gary's kids, Gary's kids, Gary's kids," were ringing in the air. It really was the year of the herd. Darren was jumping up and down and texting up a storm at the same time. Purple shirts were everywhere but even the opponents' fans continued applauding enthusiastically for the team that had just finished slaying the last of a host of Goliaths from the previous six games.

How can one be so happy and have rivers full of tears cascading down one's cheeks? The little cheerleader knew how: she was jumping up and down with a giant smile and the wettest eyes and cheeks in the crowd.

The fever of celebration wound down to a small buzz which allowed Nick Drake to corral the coach of the Buffaloes. Coach Alverson said "It has been an incredible journey. I never doubted my kids all year. Their mothers taught them well. All I needed to do was let them play basketball; encourage them to play their best until the very end, and to never give up. They never quit.

"It was always our goal. Take region, win state. I am very happy the title goes to my hometown. I can't tell you how hard these kids worked. They played beyond their potential and expectations but they never quit. They're a great group of kids. It's Tooele's first championship title in basketball. We couldn't win one when I was playing for the Buffs but these boys were the ones who did it today!"

Nick Drake succeeded in finding Cody Castle for his comments on the game, "I just like to rise to the occasion when I'm called upon," smiled Castle, whose shot will live forever in the history at THS. "I knew it would go in as soon as I let it go but the heroes were Holt, Lockie, Palmer, Hogan, Boucher, Despain, and our team! If anyone would have done less than his best we might have lost."

On the bus ride home the boys sang songs like "We are the Champions," and "We Will Rock You." Taylor Palmer said, "We were having fun then all of a sudden we saw five fire trucks with lights flashing and sirens blowing at a truck stop area about twenty miles from Tooele. The volunteer fire department had come to escort us back to town.

"Our bus followed the fire trucks back to the Wal-Mart parking lot on the north side of Tooele, and then we climbed on the five fire trucks to ride down Main Street, all the way to the Go-Fer gas station on the south side of town. When the buses and fire trucks turned around to go to the high school, we found out there was about twenty miles of cars behind us that were flashing lights and honking horns. It was amazingly incredible."

The bus with the band had beaten the bus with the players to the Tooele Wal-Mart by three minutes. Ms. Syra was overwhelmed with excitement as she hurried to inspire the band, "We have three minutes to get off this bus and get our instruments ready to play for our greatest performance!" With eyes filled with tears of happiness, she described what happened next.

"The bus with the team came into the parking lot right on schedule and the THS Band was ready to play for them. When the new state champions got off the bus their band was playing the Tooele High School Song. It was a very emotional moment and a great day for THS that I will never forget. I loved it!"

In another surprise, the Tooele gymnasium was full of students and Darren was there with about a dozen of the fastest male and female text message senders in the high school. In his new found excitement for basketball, he had text messaged them a description of every move and every basket during the championship game. Now all of them were converted to the game and shared in the excitement.

In an even greater surprise that rivaled a miracle: for the second time in the same night the THS Band had beaten the team, first, at the Wal-Mart parking lot and then at the high school gymnasium. Both times they were waiting with their musical instruments ready to burst into action when the new champions arrived.

When the players and Coach walked through the gym doors, the band started a prelude for the school fight song and Coach Alverson didn't miss a step. He hurried onto the court to face the band and students as he started signaling for everyone to join him in singing the school song. Emotions were high and again, every type of emotion was displayed between tears and smiles.

Coach praised the band every chance he got. "I love our band; they deserve the sixth man award during the entire tournament. They were a big boost to the team. When we needed a shot the most; the band was there. I give them the sixth man award. They were superb," he complimented. "One of the great things Tooele has been known for is the THS Band. Our band was awesome at the playoffs and they were a big part of today's miracle that included the school song they played tonight."

The run for the championship began with a miracle three point dagger by Castle to beat Ben Lomond and ended with another miracle three point dagger by Castle to beat Wasatch. Both times they were his only basket in the game. Along the way, Mike Holt made two dramatic three pointers at Bear River to force overtime in the closing seconds before Nash Lockie took over to ice the win in overtime. The whole team had contributed to the leadership roles down the stretch, anything less would have meant disaster for the Buffs. None of them had looked down and they had held their heads up with a clear focus on an impossible goal.

Nick Drake reported, "It was a long year for Tooele, with eight losses including a crushing 43 point defeat, no one could expect them to go this far. However, their perseverance and "can do" attitude taught by the example of Coach Alverson guided them to this accomplishment."

There were several high school teams with unimpressive records similar to Tooele's that were given hope in the upcoming 4A and 5A State Championship Tournaments.

The newspaper later named Cody Castle as the 3A State Tournament MVP even though he only took one shot in the championship game. He boldly maintained he didn't deserve the honor and that some of his teammates did. A truly unselfish Castle explained, "I just don't think I should've been given the award for my one moment. Holt and Lockie really led the team."

The 3A All-Tournament Team was:
Mike Holt, Tooele
Cody Castle, Tooele
Darin Mahoney, Wasatch
Reed Nielson, Morgan
Coby Leavitt, Snow Canyon

1st -Place Tooele
2nd -Place Wasatch
3rd -Place Morgan
4th -Place Snow Canyon

Everyone believed that Tooele was a team of destiny, and with fate and divine intervention, Tooele won the state championship. They say what makes a good coach is a coach that players will play hard and smart for. These kids played hard and smart for a coach with cancer, at some point earning the power of the Divine to come to their rescue. Their unrelenting example to others is a great contribution to society and mankind.

The heart of a champion or the determination of kids fighting for their coach cannot be measured. These kids fought for their coach and it became destiny.

> *The voice will call from deep inside*
> *It's the sound of your dream*
> *Listen to the voice of destiny*
> *Send Me an Angel –Scorpions*

> *Yes, you did your part.*
> *Your prayers were answered*
> *I sent you an angel*
> *May you never forget*
> *You were a "Team of Destiny"*
> *Haskell/Yarbrough*

Everybody pulls for David, nobody roots for Goliath.
Wilt Chamberlain

Champions keep playing until they get it right.
Billie Jean King

Talent wins games, but team work and intelligence wins championships.
Michael Jordan

Epilogue

Somewhere just beyond my reach there is
someone reaching back for me.
I Need a Hero- Bonnie Tyler

Basketball season ended and the spring sun had warmed up the athletic fields outdoors so the dark and quiet basketball court resembled an eerie ghost town but Coach Alverson was not forgotten. A rumor was circulating among the students that Coach was developing a new player as a secret weapon for the next season but he was very secretive about it and he only used the court when the building was vacant.

On a hot afternoon, one of the varsity basketball players came into the building earlier than expected from baseball practice. He could hear a ball bouncing in the gym so he peeked through the door window into the gym. Coach was working with someone so he started to open the door, but he stopped when he could hear Coach say, "Darren, don't worry. I won't tell anybody that you are coming here until you beat me at a game of "h-o-r-s-e." But if you ever win one, you better look out!"

The baseball player kept what he had witnessed confidential but he didn't forget what he saw.

The next year was the 2005-2006 basketball season. Cody Castle, Josh Boucher, and Alex Despain had graduated. Their friendship and spirit of competition was missed greatly but the rest of the team remained intact and they were a year older. Coach was back with another head of full steam but the chemotherapy treatments were taking a toll on him, not to mention the lingering cancer which had made him noticeably weaker.

Mike Holt shared his feelings as the 2005-2006 season began, "We had a while to think about being state champions, people talked to us about it, and we had championship rings to remind us. We thought we understood destiny, character, and even humility so we made a pact to go undefeated through the entire season. We played Juan Diego in our first game. They beat us! That ended our perfect season and we were already 0-1. We should have known better. Destiny isn't about being perfect and what was left for destiny to teach or give a reward for? Of course, Coach still had his blue marker and his whiteboard but he didn't need to use it. After the game, he showed it to us and it still had what he had written on it near the end of the championship game, 0-0. Then Coach said, "It's time to move forward. We can win one!"

Coach Alverson was awarded the 2005 Utah High School Coach of the Year.

The newspaper reported, "Alverson is an easy choice for the award. He has courageously battled lung cancer since November and led the underdog Tooele to the Class 3A basketball championship. He inspired his players by going through brutal chemotherapy treatments in the morning and still having the strength to coach in practices and games. The Buffaloes played his system well and won nine out of ten contests. Tooele was the underdog in the semifinals against Snow Canyon and championship game against Wasatch, but found a way to win both. He has two more rounds of chemotherapy treatments before he'll likely go through a surgical procedure on his lungs."

Coach was asked by the reporter how his illness affected his team and he responded, "It had something to do with our success. I cannot deny it. It made us closer and put things in perspective. It brought us closer together."

Darren had graduated from high school and left town to attend college but he was usually back in time for the Friday night games and he never failed to speak with Coach at any of the many games he attended. Sometimes it appeared that Coach was watching for him as he searched the bleachers from the court before the games began. One night, the Buff player who had been on the baseball team that had seen Coach and Darren practicing in the gym, asked Darren, "When you were secretly practicing in the gym with Coach last spring, did you ever beat him at a game of "h-o-r-s-e?"

Darren was never slow to respond so he quickly replied, "Of course I did, after he beat me a few hundred times. Coach is a very patient man and he taught me some good shooting techniques but there was one I finally discovered that I could use to beat him. Someday, I'll have you a game. In the meantime practice shooting the ball using just your right hand while you are answering text messages from me with your left hand."

The last two Novembers were not good for Coach: in November 2004 he learned he had cancer then on November 1, 2005, he was involved in a serious automobile accident that broke his back and a rib. These injuries in conjunction with the rapid weakening of his body due to mesothelioma forced him to use a wheelchair. His attendance at practice and games was still perfect as he continued coaching from his wheelchair. Lois became a full-time chauffeur to get him wherever he needed to be and they were always together.

A special recognition night was planned for Coach but just a few days before the scheduled game with Ben Lomond High School, Lois alerted Coach Medina that her husband had made a turn for the worse. He was fighting hard but he may not make it much longer. Medina reacted quickly to arrange the recognition night for the Grantsville game.

For the last year he was persistent and he was anxious to see the 2005 3A State Championship banner hanging in the new THS basketball gymnasium. He proudly spoke of it often, "The kids won it and it should hang forever in the gym where it was intended to be!"

The Buffs marched right through the season and on February 1, 2006 their record was 15-2. The Buffs played the Cowboys and it was "Gary Alverson Recognition Night."

For Coach, he was at Tooele High School, in Sportstown USA; he was right where he wanted to be and he was in the company of his family and his best friends.

The building was always full when the Cowboys came to town and at halftime there wasn't even any standing room left. Newspaper reporters and cameras filled the court and a microphone was setup at midcourt. Coach looked a little nervous because he didn't want to be rolled to midcourt in his wheelchair but he did it anyway. He was followed by nearly fifty family members, old high school teammates, and cheered on by more than 1,500 people in the stands. Most of them were wearing purple shirts with "The Herd" printed on the front and "Gary's Kids" on the back.

Whether he liked it or not, it was "Gary Alverson Recognition Night" at Tooele High School, and friends and family members—including his five sons, one daughter and nine grandchildren—came from all over the state to honor one of the nicest men in the state.

"He's been a wonderful husband and father, and those things are very important to him. I think he's been an exceptional good friend to a lot of people. Not only in coaching, but in our church, and some of his friends from high school," said Lois Alverson, Coach's wife of thirty-six years. "He loves all of his students and I don't know anybody who has anything bad to say about Gary."

Joining Coach, on the court were nearly all of his basketball teammates from his Tooele graduating class of 1964—as well as a handful of 1963 graduates. During the ceremony, the school retired his basketball jersey with the number "55" with a "Gary Alverson" banner above the scoreboard. Perhaps most importantly to Coach, he was excited when they unveiled a banner that said, "2005 State Basketball Champions" that his kids had won, to shine as an inspiration in the THS gym forever.

The 3A championship represented the beginning of Coach's 13-month long battle with lung cancer caused by asbestos, a battle he fought with every breath and continued to fight. He said, "The kids have become my good friends. Coaching is rewarding and there is nothing like it. In life your family is very important then religion and then it is important to have good friends around you."

Amazingly, he never missed a practice, and ultimately guided Tooele to its first basketball state championship in school history with a stunning upset against heavily-favored Wasatch.

A weakened heart made surgery too risky, so Coach underwent a few radiation treatments and continued praying for a miracle, "I can beat this!"

Through it all, he's maintained a positive outlook on life, "Difficulties make us better, not bitter!"

"He's never complained, and the fact he's never complained and said anything negative through this whole ordeal is inspiring," said Tooele guard Mike Holt.

Nash Lockie and Josh Cedar both stated in an interview, "The team had dedicated the season to Coach and we share the belief with our teammates that it helped us win the state championship."

After he broke his back and fractured a rib in a November 1, automobile accident, there was no way he was going to miss tryouts or practice as a result. So every day for the previous three months, Lois had been the designated driver on the commute from their Salt Lake City home to Tooele for practice.

On the night of his tribute, Lois said, "I've had the unique opportunity to really get to know the boys, and they really are the most fantastic group of boys."

She continued, "It wasn't until two days ago that Coach finally missed a practice. He was upgraded to a more-comfortable wheelchair and had been given a morphine drip to deal with the pain from the cancer that has spread through his ribs and into his esophagus. And like clockwork, he was back at practice today."

After the tribute, like he'd done 302 times before, he proceeded to coach his team to another victory. The win on the night of his tribute was number 303. After the game, he stood up. Somehow he walked with his own strength to midcourt and waived to the Tooele student section one last time.

The Buffs finished the night with a 59-44 win over Grantsville who shared the burdens, during the game, which had been on the shoulders of the Buffs for fourteen months.

The night will always be a reminder about the impact Coach Alverson had on people's lives. Mike Holt shared the feelings of his teammates, "I hope tonight meant a lot to him, to show him that we love him."

On a Friday, two days later, the Buffs lost to Logan High School, 39-36, in the first game Coach had ever missed at THS. He was too weak and it was best to spend the time with his family.

Early Wednesday morning, February 8, the same day as the Ben Lomond game, a beep sounded in every classroom in THS to alert the students and faculty that a message from the principal's office would follow. "Will all THS basketball players please report to the faculty lounge? This included the entire freshmen, sophomore, junior varsity, and varsity teams.

The hearts of the players and everyone within the sound of the announcement sank. Before the players could group in the lounge area, tears were already filling their eyes and they were too choked up to speak. They all knew what they were about to be told. "During last night with his family at his side, Coach died after a long battle against a vicious foe. He fought to the very end and never gave up."

Nothing could have prepared them for the emotional pain. Several minutes went by as each boy and assistant coach thought to themselves about a long string of events they had shared with Coach.

The newspapers reported:

"On Tuesday, February 7, 2006, Tooele boys basketball coach Gary Alverson, 59, passed away in his home following a fourteen-month battle with lung cancer caused by asbestos.

"Often regarded as one of the nicest guys in the coaching profession, Alverson won 303 games during a coaching career that lasted over thirty years. He coached Bonneville to state titles in 1985 and 1987, and last year coached his alma mater to the 3A title in just his third season as Tooele's head coach.

"Despite the painful side effects of cancer and chemotherapy, Alverson never missed a game until last Friday. The Tooele High School principal said after a lifetime of service coaching young men and teaching his students, he decided to spend his last days with his family.

"Last Wednesday, Tooele honored Alverson in a fifteen-minute ceremony during halftime in the game against Grantsville.

"With Alverson sitting in his wheelchair at midcourt, surrounded by well over fifty family and friends, Tooele retired his No. 55 high school jersey, as well as unveiling the 2005 state basketball championship banner."

The Ben Lomond Scots sent kind words of condolences and offered to reschedule the game but the Buffs wanted to play it anyway.

That afternoon, a few mothers stitched Coach's high school number, "55," on the top left shoulder of each player's jersey. Minutes before the

Ben Lomond game, Coach's empty wheelchair was guided to his usual position on the side of the court. Then just before tipoff each one of the Buffs placed a red rose on it.

The Buffs won the game but an atmosphere of reverence prevailed that made it difficult for the Scots as well as the Buffs to keep a game in perspective with life.

The win against Ben Lomond High School gave them the best record the Buffs ever had at this stage of the season, 17-3, and they kept moving forward and eventually into the state tournament.

To begin the tournament they beat Morgan in the quarter-finals and then Dixie in the semifinals to qualify for the 3A State Basketball Championship game. They qualified to play the powerhouse, Judge Memorial High School, and they were determined to win their second state championship in a row.

The Buffs stayed close for a while but gradually fell behind. The crowd shouted chants of encouragement, "Alverson, Alverson, Alverson," but they were exhausted; they had carried the weight of countless pressures for nearly fifteen months, they had lost the coach they loved, and they were out of gas. The Buffs couldn't catch up and the final buzzer mercifully ended the basketball game for the emotional and physically drained young men who had never quit moving forward for their coach. The score was 40-29.

This was another spectacular season in nearly a century of basketball at Tooele High School. They lost the state championship game but they still held the best THS basketball record ever, 21-4. Even though they did not win the state championship game two years in a row, they could not deny the many miracles they had witnessed during the last two basketball seasons.

Destiny doesn't intend to force anyone to be perfect during a season, in tournament play, or in life but the Buffs were a "Team of Destiny." This they understood. In championship games they weren't perfect, their record was 1-1, but in Coach's book they were still 1-0, with a lifetime ahead of them. A year earlier, just before their 2005 miracle championship game, Coach told them, "If you win tonight, you will always be 1-0."

Coach's lovely wife Lois understood and felt the same sadness the boys felt. She was a tough survivor who thoughtfully met with the team in the locker room immediately after the game. During a compassionate moment she taught and encouraged a valiant and tearful group of young men who felt as if they had let their coach down.

Like the angel she was, Lois relayed an inspiring message to them, "Coach has been with you every step of the way and he was constantly by your side tonight. He is very proud of you. Hold your heads high. You never quit. You are his champions. He will always love you and he will always be pulling for you!"

Here's a tiger to Tooele High.
May our colors ever proudly fly
We are here to stay until we die
Forever and forever in Tooele
Cheers to those who stand for us today
Tears for those we leave along the way
All good fellows we are here to stay
Forever and forever in Tooele
Rah-rah, rah-rah everybody sing
Every echo ring
Far away we leave our hearts to stay
Forever and forever in Tooele.

More than ninety years ago an author wrote the words of the Tooele High School Song. It is a fitting and accurate prophesy that was fulfilled as if he had seen this story at this very moment in time and maybe several more in his day.

Post script: In his honor THS started the "Gary Alverson Most Inspirational Player Award" and erected a cement bench and plaque outside the gym doors.

After receiving many awards, Coach Gary Alverson was inducted into the Utah Coaches Hall of Fame on May 11, 2010.

The basketball careers were soon over for every player on the team but they are still champions.

The End

Dan Garth Haskell was born January 9, 1963 in Payson, Utah. He graduated from Payson High School in 1981. In 1982-1983 he served an LDS mission in the Wisconsin Milwaukee Mission. Then he attended Dixie Junior College 1985-1987, while there he played defensive back for the Dixie Rebels. Later he graduated from Utah State University in 1989, and played one year of football for the Aggies. Dan married in 1989 and received his first coaching and teaching job at Rich High School in Randolph, Utah. After a few years as the Head Football Coach of the Rich Rebels, and undefeated J.V. Basketball Coach, Dan took a job in Tropic, Utah as the Head Basketball Coach of the Bryce Valley Mustangs. In his first year there he led them to a Region Championship, Region Tournament Championship and a number one ranking in the 1A state classification, finishing third place in state. Dan and his family moved to Tooele, Utah in 1994 coaching football and basketball at Tooele High School. Then he took the J.V. basketball job at Grantsville High School, where they won the State Championship in 1998. Dan and his wife Tina currently reside in Stockton, Utah and have six kids.

David J. Yarbrough graduated from Tooele High School in 1969 and Southern Utah University in 1973. He served in the Bangkok Thailand and the San Diego California Mission in 1977-1979. He married Heather in 1980 and they have lived in Stockton, Utah since then where they raised three sons and three daughters. David has previously authored one more book entitled "There Is Something in the Air." It is available from BarnesandNoble. com.